Driving Disruption

Jasmin

So great to

have you in class

Luv Dave 4/23/19

Also by David S. Pottruck

Stacking the Deck:
How to Lead Breakthrough Change Against Any Odds

Also by David S. Pottruck and Terry Pearce

Clicks and Mortar:
Passion-Driven Growth in an Internet-Driven World

Driving Disruption

An Operator's Manual

David S. Pottruck

Maroch Hale Publishing House · San Francisco · 2019

Driving Disruption:
An Operator's Manual

by David S. Pottruck

Published by
Maroch Hale Publishing House
www.MarochHale.com

© 2019 David S. Pottruck. All rights reserved.

ISBN: 978-1-7326364-0-8 trade paperback
      978-1-7326364-1-5 electronic book

Design and composition: www.dmargulis.com

MANUFACTURED IN THE UNITED STATES OF AMERICA

*To all my grown children
and
my grandchildren*

*May you all have the vision and courage
to drive positive disruption
and make the world a better place*

Contents

Driving Disruption: An Operator's Manual

Driving Disruption

We are continually faced with a series of great
opportunities brilliantly disguised as insoluble problems.
> —John W. Gardner, Secretary of Health, Education,
> and Welfare under Lyndon Johnson

DISRUPTIVE CHANGE—THE BOLD, BREAKTHROUGH initiative that dramatically and profoundly affects the organization and the people in it—redefines the prospects for the future. No matter how necessary the change or how seemingly evident the need, introducing and implementing innovative, disruptive change demands continuous hard work, exponentially more than that required for incremental change. And logically so. Incremental change plans often aim for 5 to 15 percent annualized rate of improvement; by contrast, when you look for change results in the realm of 30 to 50 percent improvement or more, you may well have to question assumptions that seem, to some, unassailable.

Worth it? Consider that disruptive change can increase revenues or reduce costs. It can mean a new distribution channel or a new line of products. And it can be as exciting as launching an international expansion or as scary as a massive restructuring and downsizing effort. What is an enormous change to one organization can be business as usual to another. Innovative change depends on the situation or context—and it can arrive via unexpected partnerships. Early in 2018, JPMorgan Chase & Co.,

Amazon.com, and Berkshire Hathaway announced an alliance and an initiative that could well disrupt the health care industry. With the goal of providing quality health care to the more than one million individuals employed by their companies in the United States, the organizations' leaders, Jamie Dimon, Jeff Bezos, and Warren E. Buffett, are undertaking change on a huge scale. Creating a new, simplified health care system that will fill a need more efficiently and at reduced costs, while improving employee satisfaction and loyalty? Sounds like a challenge well worth the effort, on many levels.

Whatever the scale of your change or its purpose, whether it is needed to correct your organization's vulnerabilities from other industries, to decrease costs, to maintain a competitive edge, or to benefit employees, it will undoubtedly present challenges. How then can you increase your likelihood of success?

Given how important breakthrough change is, years ago I was surprised to find that there was no resource for on-the-ground leaders seeking clear ways to develop the skills to *implement* change within their organizations, whether for profit or non-profit. Plenty of books and articles about strategic change and leading or managing change existed, many of them very insightful. Some, especially John Kotter's groundbreaking *Leading Change*, are invaluable and have stood the test of time. But where was the discussion of the practical, operational side of leading bold, transformational, disruptive, breakthrough change?

I set out to present the human reality of leading big, risky change initiatives—and in ways that could be immediately put to use. Initially, I drew on my experience: I had learned on the ground and I sometimes made big mistakes. Hindsight allowed me to realize that many of my attempts to lead change initiatives were more difficult than they had to be—and were more instructive as a result. I hoped to guide readers past the pitfalls—and I knew I hadn't seen them all. So, in preparing to write *Stacking the Deck: How to Lead Breakthrough Change Against Any Odds*, which was published in 2014, I sought advice and counsel from business leaders with a range of relevant experiences, all of whom had led extraordinary change initiatives during their careers. Our discussions expanded my thinking, challenged some of my initial ideas, and helped make my principles much more complete and robust. Together, their stories and mine provided encouragement and guidance to help readers accelerate their successes and those of their organizations.

In today's world, leaders at all levels face the challenges of change initiatives. There's no way around it: these big changes are disruptive. No matter where you are in your organization, you may find you have less support than you need and face more resistance than you anticipated. You're not alone: these realities are mirrored in the experiences of many of the interviewees. The pace and pressures of business today are such that many leaders struggle to find the time to read a lengthy leadership book crammed with stories, interviews, and new ideas. Much as I believe *Stacking the Deck* remains a useful book, full of specific, instructive stories from a wide range of leaders and circumstances, readers also need practical support, quickly. So, I recently set out to distill my original ideas, some new thinking, and feedback on the process that I've received from literally hundreds of my former students and executives with whom I work. The result is *Driving Disruption*, a streamlined and reorganized workbook or operator's manual designed to be consumed and used daily, not just read and shelved. In it, I present the combined learnings from my experiences, those of leaders interviewed before, and fresh insights from new experiences and interviews. While few interviewees are quoted in this workbook, each interview was rich with ideas that either validated my process or caused me to rethink or modify my approach in some fashion.

After this brief Introduction, the material is divided into two main parts. Part One establishes and focuses on the critical practices and higher skills that are necessary for planning and leading disruptive change. Leadership communication skills and the ability to inspire others are absolutely foundational to the entire process. For these, and indeed, for the larger picture that informs my career, I bow to Terry Pearce, leadership consultant and author of *Leading Out Loud: A Guide for Engaging Others in Creating the Future*. Without Terry's guidance and long-term coaching, what leadership communication skills I have might yet be at their most rudimentary level. In short, there is simply no one more knowledgeable and experienced.

Chapter One sets forth some of the challenges inherent in innovative change and an overview of the three interconnected essentials you need to initiate change and see it through. Chapter Two describes the practicalities of becoming a talent magnet who can readily gather the right team to get change off the ground. Becoming a truly effective talent magnet demands that you go deeper, and Chapter Three addresses the need to develop yourself as an inspirational leader and to strengthen these skills over time. Chapter Four expands on the leadership communication skills and the self-study that will prepare you for all the communication you will be presenting throughout the change, every step of the way, every day.

If you're in a blazing hurry to make change happen, you might be tempted to leap right to the steps themselves, which are delineated in Part Two. Resist that urge. Without the higher skills discussed in Part One, any attempts to lead bold change will be hindered, if not completely dead in the water. You need to be fully prepared for the long haul. Until you can develop yourself as a leader, how can you hope to draw talent to you and have followers come with you as you and your organization head into new territory?

Part Two addresses the specific steps you and your team will need to traverse as you work toward making your change a reality. This process is designed to mitigate the risks that come with change by having you take concrete actions to increase your chances of success. This preparation does not make the change less bold, nor does it guarantee success. It simply creates an advantage (more accurately, a series of advantages) that can help you overcome the real difficulties involved in promoting a change to people who are resistant if not outright fearful of it. The steps— culled from experience, shared, critiqued, tested in practice, re-sequenced, and further refined in the years since *Stacking the Deck*—provide a guide to preparing and planning so that your change initiative and your team have the best possible shot at succeeding.

The steps are presented in the order in which you should undertake them, although there are exceptions. Steps often overlap, and circumstances frequently demand that you double back to repeat or redo a previous step in the process. Change is not linear and nothing about this reality should throw you off your game plan. Preparing for and understanding the process allows you to take on big, transformative change with increasing confidence and momentum, because you know that you have a proven approach going in.

Step One is *establishing the need to change and creating a sense of urgency* around that need. Given the psychological aspect of change, this step is critical and critically positioned. Making the change necessary and urgent in the minds of those it affects most is the social and emotional foundation for everything that comes afterwards.

Step Two focuses on *recruiting and unifying your inner team* of innovation leaders who will help you define the future and make it a reality.

Step Three requires that you *develop and communicate a clear and compelling vision* of the future. This is the task that your new innovation leadership team must own.

Step Four enables you to anticipate, understand, and plan to overcome *potential barriers to success.* Inevitably, some will surprise you, and you can plan to immediately deal with the ones you anticipate.

Step Five describes how to *develop and manage a clear, executable plan* that answers all the big questions your change poses while still recognizing the uncertainty and risk involved. This step builds upon Step Two's principles for building the inner team and addresses the need to find people with the necessary skills and successfully pull them together for the broader team.

Step Six explains how to *break the change initiative into manageable pieces* to build momentum and exponentially increase your chances of success. Further, it discusses *defining metrics, developing analytics,* and the importance of actively *sharing your results* as motivational tools *to build momentum.*

Step Seven covers the power of *pilot implementations,* describes the critical differences between proof of concept pilots and scalability pilots, and introduces stacked proof of concept pilots.

Step Eight discusses how to *roll out the steps* and provides practical advice on *pulling the steps together* to bring your innovative change to the real world.

For a visual of sequencing the steps, see page 40.

Together, these steps represent a plan of action that will take you from the first realization that a change needs to be made through a complete shift in the way you implement this change. Detailed questions to consider and practices and actions to undertake are provided on www.DrivingDisruption.com. The downloadable worksheets set forth questions and action items for Steps One through Seven. They are designed to guide you through the process, give space for your ideas, and serve as a mental review every time you work through big transitions.

I've done this more than a few times and am still learning; some readings and resources I recommend are on the website. Further, in speaking, teaching, and writing about bold, breakthrough, innovative, transformative change—in short, disruptive change—I have had the unique opportunity to interact with a magnificent collection of world-class innovators from a variety of industries, company cultures, and economic environments. These people—an ever-expanding group, whose names and affiliations you will find listed on the website—have broadened my perspective enormously. You'll also find some of their stories and examples, in abbreviated form, on the website.

The Afterword considers innovation and change leadership in general, as a springboard to the future that leaders must constantly scan. My hope is that the varied perspectives and experiences will help you bridge the gap between idea and reality as you lead and implement disruptive change. Consider *Driving Disruption* as a hands-on workbook to help you understand and decode the problems, overcome the difficulties, and find the hidden opportunities. As you work on your leadership skills and undertake the steps—sometimes cycling back through them over the course of the change—you will vastly increase your chances of success in the future.

Use the margins!

Part One

Skills and Practices
for the Journey

CHAPTER ONE

Why Disruptive Change Is So Hard

MOST ORGANIZATIONS' PROCESSES AND culture are structured for predictability, reliability, control, and risk minimization. Disruptive change is the polar opposite. It is unpredictable and favors responsiveness to new realities over control and staying the course. It is inherently risky and goes against every instinct company leaders have developed over the course of their careers. Is it any wonder, then, that employees often resist such change—even in companies whose leaders say it's exactly what they need?

Every business is filled with people who depend heavily upon procedures continuing as they always have. That's what "expertise" is; you spend ten, fifteen, or even twenty years doing something a certain way and therefore become an expert in it. Your knowledge of the way things have always been done is what gives you value as an employee. So, when some brand-new executive comes in and tells you everything is about to change—but it's going to be great and you should greet it with open arms—how would you feel?

If you answered, "Pretty darn nervous" you're neither alone nor illogical. People's emotional response to a specific change initiative can be unpredictable and enormously powerful. Leaders must find ways to help people see the need for change and then inspire them to move toward it with confidence and urgency. This is a daunting struggle and one that is not easy on any side of it, as I've learned and relearned over the years.

Heading into Change

My experiences in a variety of capacities for corporations that differed in size, goals, industry, corporate culture, and more have shaped how I see change. A brief overview will give a sense of where these principles came from and the opportunities I've had to put them into practice—or failed to put them into practice.

In 1976, I began my career in financial services at Citibank, where I had my first experience in implementing breakthrough change initiatives. I went from Citi to Shearson, a traditional brokerage that was not interested in change and far more interested in sales. When I joined Charles Schwab in 1984, it was still a fairly small company. CEO Chuck Schwab and his Chief Operating Officer, Larry Stupski, were never afraid to dream big. They were brave and brilliant leaders of a team I was fortunate to join.

Originally hired as the director of marketing, I was mostly leading incremental changes, working on small improvements in the types of ads we were running, the ways we were handling our inbound inquires, and how we were measuring success. As my career grew, I had the opportunity to lead changes that were bigger, bolder, and more challenging. Circumstances and corporate culture combined to provide an unprecedented space for experimentation and risk-taking. I made my first stabs at leading bold change and discovered a lot of ways I would lead differently in the future.

There, I learned that change never, ever stops while the world advances and progresses. Competition, the marketplace, and technological advances make it necessary to keep growing and changing. And grow, we did. During my tenure, Schwab's assets in custody grew from $5 billion to over $1 trillion and the company's equity value grew from roughly $50 million to approximately $16 billion. It was exciting, intense, and often challenging. I weathered a number of storms during my two decades at Charles Schwab, but the burst of the dotcom bubble in the early 2000s caught me by surprise and I experienced firsthand what happens when you stop leading bold change. Suddenly, my job as Schwab's CEO became entirely about finding new ways to reduce costs and new places to cut. In large part, this meant directing waves of firings, downsizing a 25,000-person company by 10,000. These were people I knew well, people who had been instrumental in making the company successful. I think the Schwab board could tell that my heart was not in it. And they could certainly tell that I had stopped scanning the horizon for transformative change. I left the company in 2004 due to a combination of my own inability to continue innovating and my board's shrunken patience. Much as I wish I had responded to the downturn differently, Schwab needed more than I was able to deliver. I had stopped leading change and, instead, became a change that someone else needed to make.

Over the years, I have served on the boards of many companies: from companies in their earliest stages, to young public companies, to Fortune 50 corporations. I have seen them succeed and I have seen them stumble and fail. I've been a part of two start-ups that invested over $150 million in getting off the ground. One failed completely and the other is blossoming. As a member of Intel's board from 1998 to 2018, I've seen their successes and the challenges they've faced over decades.

Why bring up all this history? I relate this to make it clear that I know change—big and small—from the inside out and have seen successes and failures throughout my career. I've seen and made many mistakes, sometimes of judgment and sometimes of process. To a large degree, the failures did not occur because the proposed change was toxic or wrongheaded, or the effort inadequate. Instead, they were often rooted in an insufficient understanding of how truly difficult it is to overcome resistance, deal with uncertainty, respond to new facts, and execute the myriad details necessary to increase the chances for success. As a self-proclaimed change junkie, I kept at it, trying new ideas and tactics on the way to the future. By learning along the way, eventually and over time I started to succeed more and more.

Disruptive change is not easy for me, or for anyone, to implement. It is inherently challenging and tremendously difficult. Leading it will test you to your core. And yet you must persevere. As the pace of innovation accelerates, competition is becoming ever more intense. To lead bold change successfully, you must conceptualize change, overcome emotion (your own and others'), convince people to follow you, and maintain an extraordinary level of tenacity and resilience over the long haul. These are all big tasks—not one is easy. In describing not just the *what* but the *how* of change, this book will help you learn to successfully plan and effectively execute dramatic changes for the future.

The Essentials for Disruptive Change

To create the possibility for disruptive change you need a solid, well-formulated strategy for where you need to go. Many managers believe this is the hardest part of the job. It isn't.

The part that is amazingly hard and consistently underestimated, the phase in which most teams and most leaders fail, is the execution of the change. Simply stated, in most companies, processes and systems are built to reinforce the status quo and minimize risk. Therefore, the odds are against you as you set out to implement transformative change. To change those odds and tilt them in favor of the change, you must focus on three essentials:

1. Drawing together *a team with the right talent*. This is a two-pronged process, beginning with your leadership team and expanding to the broader team as you get further along in introducing and rolling out your change. It's also ongoing, as you may well add to and refresh these teams over time.

2. Developing your *leadership skills* so that you are authentic, trustworthy, and inspirational. These skills are central to everything involved with change, from planning and gathering the team all the way through to execution. Often, it is essentially the leader's resolve and tenacity that keep the people and process moving forward. The burden of this responsibility cannot be overestimated.

3. Establishing and supporting *a process that builds both momentum and the perception of momentum*. The *momentum* that develops in support of the change fuels people's energy and enthusiasm and helps carry them through the long days and hard work required. The *perception* of momentum—seeing progress and movement towards the goals—can bring others along to actively support the change. The steps of this process are closely connected, so closely that the process is actually iterative, with some steps occurring simultaneously and some recurring over the course of the project. It demands juggling and can't be one at a time; instead, you must attend to all the steps, often simultaneously. Together, the steps provide a guide to preparing and planning in advance to ensure that your

change initiative and your team have the best possible shot at succeeding.

Keep these essentials front of mind as you undertake the specific steps laid out in Part Two—and as you work through rolling out the transformative change. No one can do it alone, so you will need a truly dedicated team with appropriate talent and experience. More than that, if you are committed to being a leader of change, you will assemble many teams over the course of your career. Beyond being a magnet for talent, you must be a leader worthy of this talent. The following chapters delve into these topics.

CHAPTER TWO

Prepare for the Future by Becoming a Magnet for Talent

U NDERTAKING SOMETHING AS CHALLENGING as a bold, breakthrough change requires more than smart people willing to work hard. It requires specific skills, experiences, and track records. Be sure you are preparing for that future throughout your career. The competition for top-notch people is stiff so you need to be proactive and personal about building and maintaining your contact list—and becoming a personal magnet for talent. Create and cement connections with creative, talented, driven people—wherever they are. Make it a habit to identify people with skills or attitudes you may want on your team in the future, for in this fast-moving climate, you may need them in a hurry.

Instances will arise in which even your best people are not a good fit for the job (or they are already committed on other projects). Finding the right people can be a long process—and you can shorten it considerably by consciously developing yourself as a leader, someone other people want to work for and with. If you also cultivate a diverse range of talented people both inside and outside of the organization, you give yourself a head start.

But don't imagine you have it covered. Almost by definition, something as new as a transformative change requires new skills—and often skills that haven't yet been broadly developed or even precisely defined. You'll want to cast a wide net early, looking for diversity in the broadest possible sense. Rather than focusing only on diversity's racial, gender, or ethnic dimensions, go even further and strive for diversity from every angle, including the less visible elements of attitude, experience, focus, perspective, and work style, as a few examples. You'll also want diversity in skill sets and mind-sets, and potentially in fields that at the moment may seem unrelated to your main business. You'll want to keep diversity in mind for your dream team and for every iteration of the team.

Expand Your Reach

Ideally, you want to be able to draw on an ever-expanding pool of talented people, both inside and outside your organization. Thinking about talent and looking ahead for it, discussed in these sections, covers the logistics, the practical side of becoming a magnet for talent. But first understand that to engage the best of the best, you have to be extraordinarily compelling—not just in the compensation package you offer, but even more importantly, in the personal experience you are inviting people to share. This demands being a good leader, someone people believe in and want to follow from project to project, someone who challenges people and draws out their best. The true foundation, what brings the depth and resonance you'll need as a leader, is addressed in the next two chapters.

Looking inside the organization is your first option. Are there internal people who have been involved in change efforts in the past who could be brought into this initiative? Depending upon how that change effort played out, they may be eager for another or wary. Your reputation as a leader who challenges, develops, and promotes people will also be a huge factor. As you are developing the basic outline of your change, think about how you might interest people, why they should come to work with you on this transformation. Develop a list of where you might look to fill specific gaps; start listing names and qualifications of people you could call within your organization. Keep this as a priority, for the next step, going outside, may consume time (and funding) you don't have.

How can you further expand your options? Consider the people you meet at conferences, people who have worked with you before, people who have recently been part of high-profile change projects elsewhere. Cultivate professional relationships with them. Stay in touch and take a personal interest. If appropriate, you might offer to act as a mentor. Chances are, you'll wind up finding that you both benefit, for learning that reaches across generations and fields benefits everyone. And down the road, when you need unique talents on your team, you'll know exactly where to look. Start now with a specific, cross-indexed contact list of talented people whose skills you may want to cultivate for future opportunities and keep it updated. Even if the people on your list can't be recruited when you need them, they may well know people with the right skills who can be.

Looking outside the company is important for a balance of inside knowledge and outside knowledge. As beneficial as this can be, new people who are coming in from the outside may be seen as the leader's friends and be culturally rejected by the long-term base of the team. There are many issues to consider, from personal history to team dynamics. Ideally, the team will fill with highly motivated, very smart people with some relevant background, the right attitude, and the willingness to learn. Building this kind of team requires time and effort—and the benefits of creating a team blending insiders and outsiders will most often outweigh the challenges.

But what if you find yourself in need of people who aren't yet in your network? The internet provides access to an enormous range of talent, whether for project-based work or as new hires. You may already use LinkedIn to keep in touch with your network electronically; this and similar sites can help you locate people with the necessary skills. It's also worthwhile to cultivate some trusted recruiters. Ideally, you want to develop long-term relationships with recruiters who are well suited to tap pools of talent in your arena. They should understand your vision, your work style, and the quality of people you expect. Plus, they should know you and your organization well enough to get people, including those who aren't looking for new jobs, interested and excited about the possibility. Naturally, you may have to try a few recruiters to find one or two who are best for you. Spend time developing and nurturing that vital relationship and you'll find that you save time in the long run—and when you need it most.

Magnetize for Speed and Effectiveness

Being a personal magnet for talent is enormously helpful, both for the speed with which you can put together a team and for the ongoing quality and performance of that team. Leaders who are talent magnets find that the pieces just seem to fall into place more easily as the team develops. A strong, solid team whose members operate well together and have complementary skills enables the whole project to move faster and perform better. Of course, teamwork is also a critical component of the change effort and can make all the difference.

But no matter what the makeup of the team, you can't just put a structure in place and let it go. Even the best of teams need tending and nurturing. So check in, to be sure you have the right people, the right expertise, and that everyone's performing. You must constantly reexamine the careful balance between insiders and outsiders, between the old guard and new blood, between known and unknown quantities. To keep your team functioning, you must remain alert to what skills you and your team may lack and how well people are working together with the structure that's in place. This is particularly important when you're trying to move quickly.

As a leader, you want to be someone people seek out and who enables people to be their very best. Do so, and when you are assembling a team for a new project, you may find that people you've worked with ask to come on board. Your ability to draw people to you reflects well on you; by the same token, it is something to look for in those you hire. If a person doesn't have at least a small group of people to call and potentially bring over, that should be a warning sign since having a following is especially important these days.

Over time, as you build your own reputation as a change leader, you become a more and more desirable boss. That, in turn, allows you to reach out even further and build more connections. Perhaps some of these people then come to work with you. If they have a positive experience and your work together is successful, then you've cemented your relationship, added depth to your experience, and bolstered your reputation. Ideally, your network of contacts and your strength as a talent magnet then both expand to the next level.

Take a mental review. On a scale of zero to ten, where is your team today? What is their ability to lead, manage, recruit, inspire, sell? All of these are required if you are going to drive disruptive change. Is your team helping you or holding you back? Can today's team take you where you want to go? Change demands hardworking, smart people with the experience and skills specific to your situation. If you see room for improvement (there's rarely an "if" involved), understand that you can't change your outcomes until you are willing to change yourself and change your team. You need to keep reaching for challenges for yourself and you need to keep demanding that your team rise to each new challenge, whether it's one you've actively planned or one that the changing world has presented to you.

Consistently attracting the diverse pool of talented people in order to achieve bold transformational change is one part of the equation. The larger, more demanding part—inspiring them through the hard work of bold change—is the topic of the next chapter. Leadership skills must run deep and wide, for as leaders, we earn the privilege of leading our teams and our organizations by what we do and what we say, how we listen, and how we walk the talk of our values every single day.

CHAPTER THREE

Inspire by Communicating and Connecting

IN DEVELOPING THEIR PLANS for transformative change, executives often spend a great deal of their time behind closed doors, planning and budgeting. In some instances, they effectively hide from employees, in part to avoid being asked any questions they can't yet answer and because time is at a premium. See the problem? If executives are not putting themselves in situations that showcase their character, how can would-be followers determine if these leaders deserve to be followed? Ultimately, the willingness to follow stems from observing how leaders communicate and connect, how they demonstrate their character, how they make the changes they are advocating real to their constituents and inspire them to take action.

Leadership Communication Must Be Authentic

There is far more to being an effective communicator than most executives believe—at least when they are starting out. During the first twenty years of my career I thought I was pretty good at speaking to my teams and motivating them. In reality, I was barely scratching the surface on the skills I would need to lead the change initiatives that were waiting for me. When a major promotion forced me to realize that I was not just *underprepared* but *unprepared* for the level of leadership responsibility I had assumed, I started tackling these shortcomings.

As one of my remediation strategies, I went looking for someone to help me sharpen my communication within the company. When a colleague introduced me to Terry Pearce, a communication consultant and the founder and president of Leadership Communication, I thought I was getting a speechwriter. I had no idea what was really ahead.

For our first project together, I wanted some help with a speech I was planning to give to the 200 top executives within our then 3,500-person company. I'd never worked intensively with a speechwriter and wasn't sure what to expect. Whatever vague notions I did have were soon blown out of the water.

As I finished telling Terry the broad strokes of what I wanted him to do, he interrupted me. "I can do that, Dave, but I don't think what you have in mind is really what you want to say." Truthfully, I was taken aback. He went on. "If we really want to inspire these people, I need you to spend some time talking to me about who you are and what experiences have shaped your life. I need to know what moves you, what your values are, what motivates you when you have won and when you have lost. I need to know who you are and why you care about all of this as passionately as you do. Then we can work on this speech you have coming up."

I was flabbergasted and my response was immediate. "Terry, I'm a really busy guy. Can't we just discuss the message I want to deliver and then you find a really clear and compelling way for me to say it?" Frustration was entering my tone of voice.

Terry calmly replied, "Sorry, Dave, that's not really what I do." He continued, saying, "There are lots of people who are good with words, and sometimes that works for articles, but that's not what we need right now. Everyone knows the topic because you have been working on this change for a while. It's less about *what* you say and more about *how* you say it and whether or not it is authentic. You need to deliver a message that will be compelling because everyone understands and believes your personal commitment to what you want them to do, and that you believe it is not only in your best interest, but in their best interest as well. Once they sign up for the values embedded in what you are suggesting, their actions will follow. The facts are important, but to inspire, you must be authentic and speak from the heart. After all, they are following *you*, not just the idea. Both are important—and this is what leadership communication is all about."

Clearly, I hadn't hired a speechwriter but a communication expert and a leadership coach who deeply understood—and got it through my head—that it is the leader's ability to *connect* with people that will inspire them and earn their following. Leaders must earn people's hearts and their full engagement. Leaders must be seen as worthy, and unfailingly so; this demands that you let your character shine through. You do this by sharing stories of your successes and especially your failures, the experiences that have shaped and developed your personal values. Only then can your urgency about the change come through.

I was incredibly lucky to have stumbled into this relationship, which continued for the rest of my tenure at Schwab, and beyond. Terry is the author of *Leading Out Loud*, a best-selling book on leadership communication currently in its third edition. I consider it invaluable and assign it to all my students. Essentially all my ideas and all I know about this subject come from what I have learned from Terry's coaching and what I experienced while we were working together. When my leadership communication has been most genuine and most effective in inspiring people, it has been thanks to Terry's coaching and to his advice and reminders that have become part of me. With his blessing, I'm sharing some of that here—and trusting you to make time for his book as well.

Make Values Visible with Stories—Not Numbers

During our work together, Terry and I often revisited the idea that while facts are important, it's values and authenticity that make the difference. We understood that effective, empathetic communication, a commitment to culture building, and the character of the leader can be a foundation for a transformative change project and then contribute to making that change a reality.

Change is an emotional issue. As Terry explained, "Change can seem chaotic, senseless, and frightening—and that is why people hate it. But progress is different. It is change with an underlying worthwhile challenge and purpose." We both understood that for people to see a change as progress, "the narrative of where we are going has to look better than the narrative of where we have been." It also has to look better than where we could wind up if we don't make the proposed change. To tackle a big change or turn a company around, we need the stories and retellings of personal experiences that are forward thinking, inspiring, and that appeal to our emotional foundations.

As a numbers guy, it took me a long time to fully appreciate that if you want to overcome emotional objections, you cannot rely on facts and figures alone. It's a lesson I've had to relearn too many times. When I've forgotten it or discounted Terry's advice to "rely heavily on stories, experiences, metaphor, and image," my presentations have been relatively ineffective. Numbers may seem a faster way to make a point, but it's stories that people remember and that change the way they think and feel.

The personal experiences and stories you share with others create the emotional engagement that begins the transformation of "change" into "progress." It's how you build the purpose behind the change that gives it meaning and allows for buy-in, not just practically but emotionally as well. Unfortunately, executives—even those with the experience to know better (and I include myself here)—often fall into the trap of giving employees reams of facts, statistics, and numbers to create the case for change. This may work with your board, but if you want to encourage those whose lives and daily activities will be directly affected by your change initiative, stories are the way to begin overcoming emotional resistance and generating engagement.

This need for engagement is a constant. You can't simply demand the support of the people on the front lines. You must show that you understand what the change might mean to them. Put yourself in others' shoes, practice empathy, carefully consider and acknowledge how it may look through their lens. Help them to see the change as a positive shift for the future. Don't make the mistake of thinking that money can buy the support that you will need. *Money doesn't inspire; it motivates.* That gets you people's hands. It is *meaning* that gets their hearts, that fuels their discretionary effort. It's meaning that captures their thinking, action, and desire to be active members of the project team. It's meaning that prompts their willingness to disrupt their daily existence to do things a new way. Communicating about change is less about *motivation* (the exchange of behaviors for rewards) and more about *inspiration* (appealing to an innate desire to be a part of and contribute to something really important). Hence inspirational communication is a must for leading change.

Competence and Connection Are Key

An aside for the numbers folks out there: A Gallup survey in 1995 asked a group of executives to appraise themselves on whether or not they were inspirational communicators. Executives—an enthusiastic 93 percent of them—reported that they were "very or somewhat effective in inspiring communications." Unfortunately, only 26 percent of their followers rated them as inspirational communicators. The good news is that we're improving: Gallup's 2013 survey on the workplace indicated that 46 percent of followers "indicated their CEO is inspiring or visionary." Clearly, we need to do better, for it's the opinion of our followers that matters here.

Why the disconnect? Top executives usually get where they are because they have a high aptitude for business and they are skilled in their areas of expertise, such as accounting, technology, or marketing. They take responsibility for outcomes, they speak with clarity, and they exhibit emotional control. They are expert at what they do, good at managing in order to drive results—and they get promoted up the ranks.

Less frequently do top executives (or members of boards of directors) achieve their career success on the basis of their ability to emotionally connect with people. You can go very far in corporate life with good technical skills, a clear voice, and the ability—and willingness—to hold yourself and others responsible and accountable. But the skills required for leading change demand more. These initiatives are long and difficult, and the road to success is often paved with setbacks and disappointments. To keep the team moving forward, leaders must connect with those they lead. This means they must be—and be seen as—trustworthy, empathetic, courageous, resolute, and passionate about the mission. Employees must admire you not just for your competence but also for your strength of character. You earn the loyalty of those around you by what you do, who you are, and how you talk about what is important to you.

The world is changing. In discussing the relative characteristics of leadership candidates, boards of directors now often focus on evidence of emotional intelligence and the ability to inspire others, as well as on competencies and other work experience. Further, boards are proactively looking to ensure that candidates will neither contribute to nor condone discriminatory, disrespectful, or predatory behavior, the prevalence of which the #MeToo and #TimesUp movements have made undeniable. Perhaps we are all moving toward "and" solutions: leaders must be competent in all the traditional senses, continue to be concerned with outcomes and metrics—*and* we must be trustworthy, empathetic, and able to communicate in ways that inspire all of those around us. In looking at the impact of these principles,

Terry and I determined that competence and connection are the key indicators of the most successful leaders. Competence alone has enabled many successful executive careers. But to become authentic leaders capable of guiding disruptive change, we must be able to display our competence and connect—appropriately and respectfully—with the people we hope to lead.

Competence and connection must be evident. All too often, when we focus on how to communicate, we think of "good communicators" as people who have a certain kind of body language or who plan out their speeches in a specific way. We may be focusing on the wrong issues and aspects of leadership. Being an effective communicator demands much more than showing up at the podium on time and reading a speech without tripping over any lines. That would be easy compared to what's really needed, as unintentionally demonstrated in a speech gone wrong.

Be Fully Present

When I was at Schwab, I had a very specific way of approaching my speeches. Terry and I would work on what I needed to communicate and on the stories or anecdotes that would add power and authenticity. Terry would then write out the speech very precisely, word for word, as though I was going to use it as a script. Then I would read it aloud over and over. Eventually, I would boil it down to a few specific bullet points as memory joggers to keep me on track. If I got stuck or on a tangent, I could look at the next bullet point and move toward it. This method worked very well: I knew what I wanted to say, Terry helped with the words and images, I prepared meticulously, and I then spoke from the heart.

But sometimes I simply didn't have the time to practice enough to get to that bullet-point step. In one such case, I asked for a teleprompter so I could read the speech. I knew it was well written and strong; the words were beautifully chosen to articulate the points we wanted to make. I expected to be just as effective reading it as I would have been speaking from notes, maybe even better. At least, that was my theory.

After the speech, I asked Jan Hier-King, a member of my executive team, whom I valued highly because I knew I could always count on her to tell me the truth—even a difficult one—what she thought of my speech.

She didn't mince her words. "Horrible," Jan said immediately. "I hated it. You delivered the speech pretty well, but we could tell that you were reading it. It didn't come from your heart and it didn't sound like you. You know," she added, "it's about how you make us feel. Your authentic display of passion and emotion energizes us. That's what makes a good speech. This didn't work, Dave."

Jan was right, and I was wrong in thinking the words themselves would be sufficiently compelling. Terry and I had a metaphor for the error: "You got the words, but you didn't get the music." No speechwriter can do that; you have to call it from yourself. If you're lucky, you'll have trusted advisors to help you and remind you. If you're lucky, you'll quickly learn that thorough preparation is essential and that simply reading a speech is not effective (and can be counterproductive). People need to hear your passion and belief. That emotional connection is key if we are to move people to listen and pay attention rather than simply be in attendance during our speeches. It boils down to this: be prepared—and speak from the heart. It is your authenticity rather than brilliant wordsmithing that people will be moved by and remember.

Read the room – not your speech – and speak from the heart.

Of course, we must think seriously about what we want our speech to do, the kind of impact we want it to have, the action we want people to take when they leave the room. This is the heart of the issue: what do we want people to feel, to believe, and to do after our speech? Are people going to leave the meeting ready to run through the wall and take on the whole world? Or are they going to shake themselves awake and trudge over to the next meeting? If you cannot connect with people, then your ideas—no matter how important and how well thought out—will fall into a black hole.

Even if you think your idea is so good it can sell itself, take a step back and remind yourself that sitting in an audience, sometimes for hours on end, listening to a series of speeches can be difficult for people who are more used to an active workday. And no matter how well delivered those speeches are, the audience members have work waiting for them. Before speaking to a large audience, first consider the question, "Is there some reason why these people might not really pay attention to what I am about to say?" Was there a recent article, web post, or even a broadly circulated e-mail that stirred things up? If so, acknowledging this right up front can be an effective element of your talk. If you're not aware of any specific issue, then even addressing the length of the meeting can help. Starting with something as simple as,

"I know I'm the last person between you and lunch, but in the next 25 minutes I have something to cover that I believe is very important to our future success," can lead you and your audience effortlessly into your topic.

A speech is a slice in time, one that warrants extraordinarily thorough preparation. It can have a powerful impact if it resonates, sparks interest, and moves people to action. Speeches are visible and important components of your role as a leader. Successful leaders are conscious of that role in every single communication, every interaction, every venue, throughout the organization and beyond. How do you prepare for that?

Think about the level of energy and passion you bring to the table every day. Are you demonstrating a sense of urgency in everything you do? Everyone is watching you. The employees are feeding off your energy and commitment. Recognize that people don't just follow ideas; they follow people they believe in. You must be one of those people. Don't imagine you can accomplish this with a speech, an e-mail, or even a blizzard of postings. Certainly, e-mail and other electronic communications are effective—to a point. But I do know that *we earn the right to communicate electronically by the quality and frequency of our face-to-face communications.*

We must reinforce the purpose and the connection to the culture over and over again. We must imagine our employees' concerns and see the issues from their perspectives. We must remind ourselves that as we give animated, persuasive talks about the next new thing, much of our audience may be barely listening as they mentally try to answer the questions in their heads: "What does this mean to me . . . my career . . . my bonus . . . my family . . . my colleagues . . . my future?" Leaders must communicate over and over again to reach the audience where they are.

Doing so helps earn trust. And in connecting the change to the culture, leaders can reinforce the ideals of the culture. The best way to inspire these ideals is to role-model them yourself and celebrate others in your organization who do so. If you want your role to grow, you have to grow. The next chapter provides further detail on how you can improve your leadership communication skills and take them to a higher level. It also includes a framework that you can use in the process of becoming more effective as a leader.

CHAPTER FOUR

Leadership Connection Is a Discipline

IMAGINE IF YOU COULD think through every aspect of every communication scenario and prepare for it, in advance. Terry Pearce created a framework that encourages change leaders to do just that, developing a "Personal Leadership Communication Guide" in preparation for and as part of each significant change effort. In that process, you consider scenarios and write, just as you would a journal, except you do it in discrete pieces. Like a journal, you add to it with some regularity.

Terry and I have used his Guide, the framework for which appears at the end of this chapter, in our most successful efforts together. It acts as a reminder in any venue or medium, in spontaneous as well as planned situations. Further, working on it sets the stage for your internal process to unfold. Once you have thought through the Guide's concepts—competence, trustworthiness, context, the future, and commitment to action—and put your thoughts to paper, you will find the concepts and practices will come automatically to mind when you need them, as will the personal and relevant stories that support them.

The Guide itself is not going to transform you into a leader any more than playing scales can make you a great pianist. What counts is what you put into it and grapple with as you consider what has shaped you, what is important to you, and what you see for the future. It provides a chance to ask yourself some fundamental questions about who you are and what you see ahead:

- What accomplishments have made you proud?
- What failures have taught you the most?
- What kinds of changes do you want to be involved with?
- What are you doing?
- Why exactly does this matter to you?
- Why should it matter to others?

It takes discipline to tackle these questions on your own. In fact, it takes discipline to tackle them even in a structured environment or with a coach. And tackling them as you're simultaneously faced with the crushing pace of business can seem impossible. But make the time. Allowing yourself to ponder the questions will add depth to your perspective and to your ability to connect with others.

Power versus Influence

Too often people discuss leadership in terms of power. In business, we are told we need to become powerful, have power over others. But is that what leaders actually need? I don't want people to take action or behave in certain ways because they fear me, or just because I am their boss. I want people to take certain actions toward the goals we've set—to *feel compelled* to do so—because they too believe that these goals are worth striving for.

At a fundamental level, leaders and followers have to be talking about and focused on the same goals. This speaks to a basic idea about communication: you have to consider others' perspective. It's not about what you say; it's about what they hear. And what you think you are saying can often be very different from what others are hearing.

How best to connect with the people you want to lead? In laying the groundwork for bold change, you have to first establish the need and a sense of urgency. Of course, you must have facts that support you, but for people to get drawn in and be convinced of the need for action, they first must believe *you*. You therefore need to make it personal, to involve people with stories that make the need real. Drawing on your life experiences inside and outside of work helps connect you more effectively. Doing so enables you to find the words; those questions you tackled enable you to find the music as well, which will resonate in others.

Your perspective comes from how you view the world and who you are as a person. It is molded by the sum total of your experiences and your beliefs. Becoming a good communicator requires that you uncover your own point of view and that you share it with others. Describing your point of view can be an intimidating proposition—and it is well worth the effort.

As you work on your Guide, you may wonder: "How much of this am I willing to share with others? How much am I willing to reveal of myself?" The Guide itself is for your eyes only. The stories you do share are part of what connects you to others, makes you real, and gives you believability. Sharing stories of challenges or failures in your background can be powerful—if you're willing to reveal them honestly. It can be scary to get up in front of a group of people and talk frankly about your mistakes— even old ones. But it is how you make yourself real to others. I could tell a dozen stories in which I had a lot of success and no major problems, but it is the one story of a total fiasco that will show I have the ability to admit and analyze mistakes, adjust, and learn from them. That one story will do more to establish my credibility and character than the dozen uneventful tales of triumph.

An added benefit of using stories to establish a connection with people is that in telling these stories you will relive them and feel some of their emotion again. The people you are talking with will see that you are really feeling something, and they will connect with those actual expressions of emotion. As you cultivate an atmosphere of authentic and appropriate personal connection, you build the authentic connection you are striving for as a leader.

People are looking for certain qualities and character traits in their leaders: courage, generosity, humility, integrity, resolve, responsibility. They want to know that you are capable of these personal qualities, and you need to show them, again and again. As leaders, we must earn respect for our personal character every day. In the process of sharing who you are and why you believe what you do, you can be incredibly inspiring to others.

Spreading the Message

Communicating to the team and the broader community of employees is not a one-time event. Leaders must remain visible and engaged, whatever the circumstances. Communications must be frequent, well thought out, and well received.

Leaders understand the importance of articulating the objective nature of the change and convincing those around them of the urgency involved; they also understand how critical it is to have that certainty on a gut level. If you want to be believable, you have to believe. If you don't have faith in the change you're proposing, if you don't genuinely believe that it is the best—or only—course of action, you won't be able to convince others.

In today's world of electronic communications, it might seem easier than ever to communicate to your organization. After all, there are plenty of options for reaching people electronically; this can be done instantly and made specific for each group or person. Unfortunately, connecting is not that simple. A personal presence is vital since most of us are wired to read facial expressions and body language. We read and interpret people's movements and expressions, along with the words they speak, to take in what they are communicating to us. When we are deprived of that additional sensory information, when we don't see the person, don't hear inflections, then we can't hear even a whisper of the music (as Terry and I would say) and we have a much different experience of the very same words.

I don't suggest you ignore the enormous efficiency and simplicity of electronic communication, but I do caution that you recognize its limits. It is too easy to misinterpret tone and emotion when all we have are the words in print or on screen. Particularly when the topics revolve around change and asking people to commit to change—concepts that provoke emotional responses— people require as much context as possible. No matter how precise or well intended, words alone are dangerously prone to being misunderstood and misinterpreted.

 Electronic communication is a tool for communicating *information*—not for inspiring *passion*. There is simply no replacement for standing in front of people and delivering your message in person, speaking from the heart, and never reading a speech.

The Power and Importance of Effective Listening

Any discussion of communication must include effective listening, a key skill at all levels. Unless you, as a leader, are open to new ideas and demonstrate that you want honest, candid, unfiltered input and feedback, you may get less and less of either as time goes on. People may say little rather than risk being considered brownnosers or putting their jobs in danger. This problem only increases at the higher levels. Creating an environment where everyone—including the CEO—gets and gives open and honest feedback is critical to success. Sometimes people need training and practice to get comfortable with this.

Whether it's absorbing feedback or new ideas, it is not always easy to simply listen with a fully open mind. We all know people—maybe ourselves—whose lips are pursed as they mentally frame their response before the person speaking has even finished. Does that behavior leave you with a feeling of having been thoughtfully heard? Hardly. We must come to the conversation curious. If we're truly open to people's ideas, we don't just want them to *feel* heard: we want them to *be* heard. That means we listen thoughtfully; we ask follow-up questions for clarification, depth, and detail. It requires us to show up with the humility to recognize we don't know all the answers, or even all the questions. It requires us to acknowledge that others have important ideas and thoughts to add to our thinking, even if those include objections to our whole idea. Before leaders can help people move forward toward the new, they must first take the time to hear people's resistance and their concerns.

You must prepare yourself to hear—and to want to hear—upsetting, frustrating, and even counterproductive information. Even if this happens right in the moment when your own sense of urgency is telling you, "There's no time for this!" you must make the time and be fully present and aware. This may not be easy for you; it has never been easy for me. And I know that when I muster the patience to engage in this process and be a more effective listener, I learn things I need to know and I am more effective as a leader. It's a lifelong journey.

Every aspect of leadership requires effective listening; question and answer sessions and less formal interactions are no exception. When you open a presentation to questions from your audience, there is an assumption that the answers you give are unscripted and authentic. The truth is somewhat more nuanced, since leaders can foresee that a number of fairly obvious questions will be on people's minds. Will there be layoffs? Will there be benefit cuts? How will this affect the promotional calendar? Will locations be shut down?

You can choose to proactively address the main concerns in your presentation or you can leave them for the Q&A session. Just be prepared for these questions and many others that aren't so obvious but might pop up. Good preparation means you have already considered a broad spectrum of possible questions and have thought through how you would answer them, perhaps even rehearsed this part of your presentation, just as you rehearsed the speech itself.

These sessions are also a chance to build your culture of open and honest communication. Years ago, in a Q&A session of a few thousand employees, someone asked me a particularly challenging question that put me on the spot. The question was phrased along these lines: "I noticed in the proxy that you and other top execs received multimillion-dollar bonuses last year. How does this square with the culture of economy and expense control you were just speaking about?"

A hush fell. No doubt some employees thought this employee had just stepped on a career land mine. It instantly seemed as though everyone was watching alertly to see and hear my response. Fortunately, this was a variant of a question I had anticipated, so it didn't catch me off guard or put me on the defensive, either in my physical stance or my tone. I paused for a breath and said, "I'm sure many of you must be wondering the same thing, so I thank you for putting this issue on the table and giving me a chance to describe how the board's compensation committee process works. But first, let's give this brave employee a standing ovation for having the courage to ask a question that was on a lot of people's minds!"

This employee gave me a chance to not only clarify the issue but make a deposit to the culture bank and reinforce the value of honest and open communication that we believed in. Instead, had my words, tone, or body language been combative or dismissive, if I had not yet absorbed the ideas of listening for more, I could have undermined our cultural values and ensured that in the future no one would trust me enough to offer their truthful opinion.

If we are going to demand full commitment from our people, we must demonstrate it for them. We must be leaders whose character and plans are worthy of being followed. We need to constantly reiterate what we are doing, why we are doing it, why it matters to us. We need to ask ourselves, as Terry once asked me, "Who are you, what do you want, and why?" These were not meant as rhetorical questions but as existential questions. They were the very foundation for how I needed to communicate as a leader.

Communicate Authentically

I was enormously fortunate to have been coached by the best. But what if you don't have a coach or a mentor and you find yourself in a time crunch, constantly? Were you hoping that simply answering the few questions at the beginning of this chapter or glancing over the Guide's framework would be enough? What if you also looked ahead to Step Three's action items and their concrete steps of communicating about change? The true answer is no. The action items will help with the practicalities of moving forward, on track and engaged. It's doing the harder work of Terry's Framework for Personal Leadership Communication Guide © that will take your preparation to a much deeper level.

Consider the Guide thoughtfully and use it as a tool for your own authentic self-examination, and you will have a strong foundation for every communication situation you encounter. The effort you put into constructing your Guide will cue your mind and emotions to enable you to tailor your communications appropriately for your audience. In doing so, think carefully about the impact your words can have, whatever the venue or the format. And remember, as Maya Angelou has often been quoted as saying, "People will forget what you said, people will forget what you did, but people will never forget how you made them feel." That gets to the heart of the issue and is a lesson for leaders at all levels.

The work and self-reflection you put into the Guide will help you approach communication authentically and are crucial to your ability to connect and inspire. The Guide's purpose is both internal—exploring what is important to you and why—and external—explaining what we need to do to arrive at the clear and vibrant future you are proposing. What you write as you develop your Guide will become the foundation for your communication. Your Guide will evolve over time, as you modify and supplement it with relevant new experiences and material. Your efforts will enable people to sense your passion and conviction and have a sense of your character.

The Guide presented here is simply the bare bones and no substitute for fully absorbing *Leading Out Loud*, in which Terry devotes an entire chapter to each of the Guide's four main sections and walks you through the process. The advice and the background Terry's book provides are absolutely critical to authentic leadership. If you aspire to lead, be sure to read it.

Framework for Personal Leadership Communication Guide ©*

1. Establishing competence and building trustworthiness
    - Competence
        - Clarity of purpose
            Problem
            Specific change advocated
            Evidence of compelling need
            Broad implications; value represented
        - Credentials and vulnerabilities
    - Trustworthiness
        - Displaying empathy
            Expressing gratitude
            Acknowledging resistance
            Finding commonality in purpose
        - Willingness to be known
            Personal motivation, personal value
2. Creating shared context
    - History
    - Priority
    - Current reality (include barriers)
    - Reinforcing competence and trust
    - Articulating a broader perspective
3. Declaring and describing the future: an act of creation . . .
    - Vivid picture, sensory-rich images
    - Stakes (If we do . . . If we don't. . . .)
    - Values expressed either way
4. Committing to action
    - Steps (organizational)
    - Personal commitment, personal action
    - Request for action (specific)

---

*   © Guide copyright, Terry Pearce, 2013. All rights reserved.

Part Two

Leading Disruptive Change, Step by Step

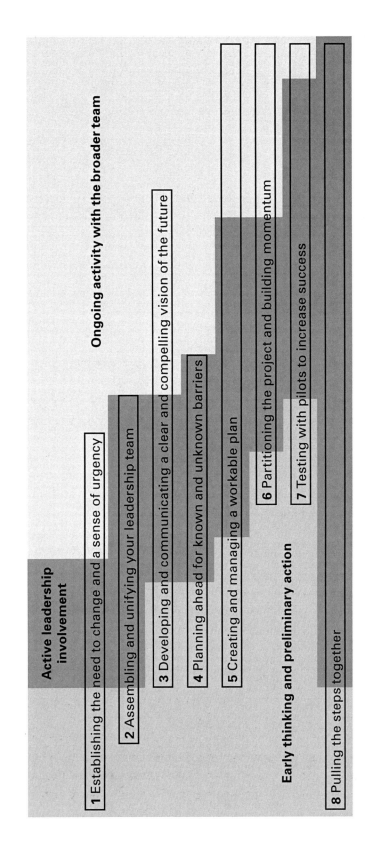

Active leadership involvement

Ongoing activity with the broader team

Early thinking and preliminary action

1 Establishing the need to change and a sense of urgency

2 Assembling and unifying your leadership team

3 Developing and communicating a clear and compelling vision of the future

4 Planning ahead for known and unknown barriers

5 Creating and managing a workable plan

6 Partitioning the project and building momentum

7 Testing with pilots to increase success

8 Pulling the steps together

Sequencing and Coordinating the Steps

Establishing the Need to Change and a Sense of Urgency

NO MATTER HOW WELL leaders understand the need for change, the challenges in driving disruptive change are enormous. Change is part of life. Yet in life and in business, some people embrace change and others actively avoid it. Change represents the unknown, and people—some of whom you must lead—almost always find the unknown scary. As Terry Pearce has often said, "People hate change. People love progress. The difference is purpose." These words offer an excellent starting point for any discussion about change. Progress implies an improvement, a move forward. And nothing progresses by staying the same.

In leading bold change, we must first convince others—those to whom we report and those on our team—that our proposed change has a positive, necessary, and urgent purpose, that it is actually progress. It can be particularly hard to convince people about what isn't obvious to them or already reflected in the hard numbers. Often leaders must convince people that staying put will eventually lead to failure. Perhaps you've seen that an erosion of competitive position has begun or is close on the horizon—and others have not yet noticed. Or there's a potential loss of a compelling opportunity to grow. Huge, obvious problems that are clearly threatening might seem easier to communicate. Even so, established companies such as Borders, Blockbuster, Tower Records, and Toys "R" Us were left behind in the wake of the internet, Amazon, and iTunes. Today, shopping malls are searching for ways to reposition themselves and retail stores are closing many of their physical locations. The "clicks and mortar" integration we discussed back in the 1990s is beginning to accelerate, with Amazon's purchase of Whole Foods as one example.

Link the Purpose and Mission

To be convincing and to draw people to your leadership team, you have to be clear about the problem or opportunity you are tackling. You will be most successful when you tie the change to the company's mission and show how the change will help achieve it.

If you are rolling your eyes at this reference to the importance of the company's mission, you are not alone. Even though nearly every company has a mission statement that is communicated to all employees from virtually the day they enter the company, and perhaps even in the recruiting process, company mission statements often become a joke among employees. In many companies, mission statements simply *exist* and aren't honored. In these cases, tying the proposed change to a mission that no one believes the company leaders really care about is doomed from the start.

Every executive I've interviewed underscored the critical importance of employees believing in and feeling connected to the corporate culture. These executives each work hard to establish and maintain a strong company culture—the values the company lives by, the actions that make those values real, and a mission that inspires employee passion and commitment. They understand that when employees believe in a mission, they get excited and passionate about contributing to the company's goals. Thus, connecting an innovative change to the company mission and explaining how it contributes to the mission can help employees see and appreciate why a change may be necessary—even critical—to the company's future success.

Whatever the purpose of the change you are proposing, convincing others of its necessity requires effort—probably more effort than you expect. Just because the need seems logical and inescapable to *you* doesn't mean that others will necessarily recognize its importance at first. No matter how long you've been facing the issues and planning the change, you have to make the case in a compelling and thoughtful way. Even so, not everyone will come on board. While you don't need all the employees on your side, you do certainly need some. For that, you must find the strength to move forward and win over the ones that you can. Getting into their shoes will help.

Understand the Big Picture—and All Perspectives

When it comes to convincing others, understanding your audience's perspective is paramount. When I took over the branch network at Schwab and began instituting what I thought were small changes, it didn't occur to me that I would need to make a special effort to get the men and women in the branch offices on board. It was clear to *me* that the changes were urgently needed; but it took a long while for me to realize that it sure wasn't clear to the average branch employee. Our perspectives were very different, in part because I had access to information that branch employees did not.

I had noticed early on that Schwab's corporate culture was wary of sales—almost anti-sales, in fact. Having come from Citibank and Shearson, where selling was perfected to an art form, I found this quite a shift in gears. Schwab used a direct-response advertising model (with a tagline of "No salesman will ever call") to attract new business: the company ran ads and waited for customers to respond. The culture permeated our branches, making our field organization fundamentally reactive rather than proactive.

At that point, Schwab's advertising was doing well and was bringing in people off the street to open new accounts. We had products that people wanted and our marketing succeeded in engaging people. Yet our engine of growth—direct-response advertising—was growing less effective as more discount competitors copied our model. If we didn't find another arrow in our growth quiver soon, our success would start to slide. The leadership team understood that this was a serious and urgent issue. The question became how to grow and be proactive (versus "sales-y") without undermining our customer-centric culture.

When I first proposed initiatives for proactively contacting customers, I thought the ideas seemed easy to implement and not that complex. Making an outbound "Welcome to Schwab" call to those who had recently opened new accounts seemed like a natural expansion of our staff's existing job description, which already included answering inbound calls, and our executive committee was very supportive of this "small change."

To me, the difference between selling and what I was proposing seemed clear. It wasn't hard-core selling to simply point out to our customers that we had IRA accounts or that our customers should start thinking about retirement funds. It was basic customer service. Our customers should know that we offered mutual funds and bonds in addition to stocks. The more-engaged customer outreach would help customers better understand what Schwab did and the benefits of opening additional accounts and depositing more money with us. At that point, our average client account was $7,200, a small fraction of the client's investable assets. There was a huge upside in encouraging clients to do more business with us; it was a good business decision, good for our customers and good for us. How hard could it be?

Anticipate Fear and Understand Its Impact

Surely at least some of the branch employees and managers would jump at the chance for a more challenging, more interesting job that would eventually provide a better rate of pay. We were offering them a chance to forge relationships with customers and take on more responsibility. But I initially failed to realize that the employees I was attempting to lead liked their jobs just as they were. As far as they were concerned, we weren't simply adding some duties to their job descriptions. We were *fundamentally changing* what they did to something that they expressly did not want to do. Many employees interpreted our proposed changes as a step toward becoming salespeople. For them, our grand plan wasn't an upgrade at all. It was a nightmare!

By most measures, Schwab was already growing and succeeding; they may have wondered, why change? What they didn't realize was that change was coming for them either way. Chuck Schwab had bigger ambitions for his company and knew that we needed new approaches. We had to do more to set ourselves apart from all the competition—and we had to do it quickly if we wanted to maximize our success.

There were plenty of implementation mistakes in the process. One was allowing the situation to be framed as a contrast between doing things as they'd always been done versus changing to something unproven and unappealing. Another was not helping the employees see all the client benefits of this enhanced way of doing business. In retrospect, this situation would have been a perfect candidate for the kind of pilot implementation discussed in Step Seven—but I hadn't learned that yet. Perhaps the most critical mistake was failing to understand the importance of presenting this change as absolutely necessary and urgent—and tied to our mission. I did neither, and as a result we struggled. My efforts to sell this vision of the future did not overcome employees' fears or their reluctance to support this change.

Hindsight makes it clear: I should have recognized and understood the fear and inertia that had hold of many employees. These people knew how to answer phones, how to react, and how to do everything we'd ever asked of them. They were comfortable in their roles. They didn't know if they would be good at making outbound calls or creating relationships with customers, and they worried that their jobs would be in jeopardy if they couldn't. They had spent years building up experience—and value for themselves as employees—and here I was, about to take it all away. Changing their job descriptions meant potentially busting everyone back down to the same level of expertise. No wonder they were fearful.

That kind of fear is powerful and visceral; it's a purely emotional response. And many leaders go wrong in attempting to counter an emotional response with data or statistics. In *The Charisma Myth*, author Olivia Fox Cabane discusses how psychology is interwoven with business principles. She explains that challenging someone's identity—as I was doing by altering Schwab's branch network—is so fundamentally threatening that sometimes the person completely and involuntarily stops listening in a physiological fear response that effectively causes the brain to disengage from what is being said.

People who are afraid do not behave logically, and they don't respond to logical appeals. Why do drowning people accidentally take their would-be rescuers down with them? Often, they're simply so terrified that they're unable to listen to directions that will help, not hinder, their rescue.

Whether a change is simply low on employees' priorities or so dramatic as to require significant effort, how can we smooth the way? What can we do to win over people who are in the throes of powerful emotions? First of all, repetition is important. It's not enough to announce a change and call it a day. You must give your employees the information again and again. Tell them in person, tell them in writing, and tell them electronically. Tell them one-on-one and tell them in big groups. It's very likely that not everyone will hear you correctly the first time. Transformative change simply cannot be accomplished with a single meeting or e-mail blast. You'll need stories that inspire and that people will remember. Prepare yourself to listen carefully and receptively to people's questions and concerns. The process will be harder than you imagine and require all the patience and resolve you can muster.

Underscore the Urgency—and Prepare for Resistance

Before you decide to convince anyone else about the change you are proposing, you have to satisfy yourself that change is not just necessary; it's necessary sooner rather than later. You must be willing and able to inspire your team. You have to invest in the change and commit to it with your time, your energy, and your budget. It is not enough to think that the numbers look good: you must truly believe in the purpose behind the change. Be sure that you've considered these issues and that you've honestly pondered and answered the following questions:

- Have I evaluated the numbers for different scenarios? Do they look good?
- Do I truly believe in the purpose behind the change?
- Am I fully convinced of the urgency of the change itself?
- Can I demonstrate that this change is worthwhile and imperative?
- Do we really have to do it *right now*?
- What will occur if we postpone it?

If you have come to a carefully considered conclusion that this change is urgently needed, then you will need to drive the change forward with all the energy and conviction you can muster. Along the way, be alert to resistance and address it.

It is easy to assume that resistance occurs primarily with the frontline employees—but that's not necessarily the case. If what you're proposing is big and bold and strategic, chances are that you will encounter people at all levels of the organization who think it may be easier to do it later. These people may voice their objections by saying, "Let's think about this some more" or "Shouldn't we get some more data?" You might also hear, "Are we moving toward the bleeding edge?" These may well be valid points, but they may also be more comfortable ways of expressing the feeling that "I'm sorry, but I just don't have it in me to risk that much or work that hard."

Understand the feeling—and know that leaders are bound to face risky changes and resistance. That's part of the job. Overcoming that resistance and maintaining momentum require constant effort. And no matter how big the successes, the need to innovate is a constant, no matter what the business. This book's website, www.DrivingDisruption.com, provides additional resources. The steps and the effort you put into the action items will help you along the way, as will the knowledge that driving change is bound to be difficult. Scan the QR code in the margin with your tablet or phone to go directly to the action items, step by step.

~~~~~

You will often face situations in which you could put off a change, but procrastinating will sacrifice certain important benefits. The sooner you take the initiative, the bigger the rewards often are. If you are catching wind of a new opportunity before any of your competitors, it may take them years to respond and catch up. True, it will be easier for them to make their own breakthrough changes after you have forged a new path. But the lead and the momentum you will have achieved may make catching up to you a daunting proposition. Time and money are two of the three great variables in any business venture, and it will cost your competitors both if they want to advance to your new level.

The third and most important variable? People.

Members of the leadership team must fully understand and share the sense of urgency, for these are the people you rely on for day-to-day success. They must not be allowed to play for time or just pay lip service to the need for change. Be aware that even within a carefully chosen team, you may find a huge amount of resistance from your inner circle. Listen, and be sure you understand the reasons, for there may be valid issues there to address. But if the resistance comes out of fear or inertia, these people must be won over or replaced. Bold initiatives require a strong and dedicated team, a team that can work together to develop, strengthen, and maintain momentum. Step Two provides guidance on assembling and building that team.

Assembling and Unifying Your Leadership Team

I F YOU ARE PROPOSING a large-scale change, you are undoubtedly passionate about how necessary it is, and busy crafting a vision for the future. And no matter how compelling the need and how strong your passion about the change required, achieving and sustaining bold change require much more. No great change has ever been accomplished by one leader alone. An individual's skill, charisma, and sheer energy are simply not enough: leaders must rely on a well-balanced leadership team. Some have the luxury (and responsibility) of hand-selecting this team. Some are brought in to work with an existing group that may or may not already function as a team. Whether you've recruited your own team, inherited one, or some combination of both, it's your job to actively develop and unify this group to guide the organization in making your change a reality.

Asking people to come on board is asking them to sign on for something that is, by its very nature, going to be hard. A big change is almost always going to require more resources than you initially believe. It will take an enormous amount of time and energy, which has to be mustered against long odds and over a long period. Since breakthrough change is outside the range of incremental changes and often well beyond the comfort zone, the leadership team must include people who are convinced that this change is both economically and strategically important, well worth overcoming the barriers and challenges ahead.

Whether in established organizations or in the start-up world, the people who are inspired and fulfilled by being a part of something new, challenging, and important are often the most successful in initiating change. Why? It sparks their imaginations and makes them feel part of something much larger and greater than themselves. These are the people you need, the pioneers who are comfortable with the risks involved.

Find and Nurture the Pioneers

In driving disruptive change, you must be able to inspire passion in the members of your team and feel confident that they are in turn capable of kindling that spark and dedication in others. The entire team must be on board. When you are creating your leadership team and looking for people to help you make this change happen, consider four key elements: skill, experience, enthusiasm, and team fit. Naturally, you want to select people with specialized skill sets and experience in the kind of project you're undertaking. Attitude, as reflected in character, enthusiasm, and team fit, is critical when it comes to change. The surprising truth is that enthusiasm and team fit may be the most challenging elements to locate.

You need people who are willing to enter unmapped terrain. These pioneers will guide your larger team, usher your change into reality, and serve as ambassadors to the rest of the organization. Having many of your core group of excited believers come from current employees already embedded within the corporate culture can be extraordinarily helpful. Your believers are the ideological "early adopters" who can form the all-important bridge between management and the people on the ground who may be skeptical of the change you are driving.

Be sure to devote enough time and energy to forming the team. As you bring new people in, you must constantly balance many variables. Do you have a team full of extroverts? Introverts? Leaders? Followers? Quick deciders, or more-reflective types? Just as you want to pull together a group of people who can work together productively, you also want to pull together a set of disparate experiences and skill sets that can mesh effectively. You may feel rushed to get the change moving and be tempted to gloss over team formation. Be warned: countless transformations have stalled out or even collapsed because very smart, highly motivated, enormously dedicated people thought that those characteristics would translate anything they attempted into success. We all want to believe that if we're smart enough and work hard enough, we can do anything we put our minds to. In my experience and the experiences of all the people I've interviewed and known, this is almost never true. Attitude *is* critical; and it's not sufficient. Leaders must find people with the *relevant* experience, and very often—particularly with innovative change—that means going outside to recruit people with key talents.

Adding one or two new people from outside the organization can also strengthen the team. The experiences—whether successes, failures, or both—that new people bring to the mix can benefit the group and facilitate the change. Yet bringing in new talent, especially a new executive, does carry risks. Cultural adaptation can be a delicate and perilous process, so be very cognizant of potential interpersonal issues as well as the attitude of any new hires.

In an ideal world, you would have the time to get a clear sense of character before hiring someone. Unfortunately, the skills we need don't always come perfectly packaged with a great personality, character, and a team-first mentality. When a huge, challenging initiative is staring you in the face, the temptation may be to recruit someone with hard-to-find skills while overlooking what may be questionable character traits. It's only natural: when you find a candidate with the skills you desperately need, you don't want to find any reasons not to hire that person. If the new hire then gets off to a shaky start with the team, it's easy to chalk it up to adjustment jitters rather than face the fact that you may have made a hiring mistake. However, it is always better to identify these problems early and deal with them before they fester, since without intervention the problems will get worse.

A toxic person who does great work and a challenging person who requires a unique hothouse atmosphere may each make you look good for a while. But even with counseling and training, people under pressure often default to old, negative habits. Let this go on too long and your leadership will soon be called into question: what kind of leader sacrifices the unity and cohesion of the team? Do corporate values matter or not? The reality is that making compromises on character to get the required skills rarely works out. So be sure to get a clear sense of character before hiring someone—and if you make a mistake, deal with it quickly. Of course, there is a difference between someone who is never going to be a team player and someone who is simply on the wrong team. It's reasonable to try a new situation for someone whose fundamental attitude, level of commitment, and work product merit the benefit of the doubt.

Take Steps to Unify the Team

Even with the right people, you have to unify the team and manage your people in the right way. True teamwork—real, effective cooperation and communication between team members—is rare and provides a huge edge when embarking on a big change initiative. More than the plans you develop or the financial resources at your disposal, it's your *people* and the way you manage them that will make the difference.

How you behave as a leader and as a team player is critical and too easily overlooked (but not by the team). Although most people describe themselves as team players, this often means, "I love teams, as long as they follow all of my suggestions." Much as I hate to admit it, that quote could have been mine in the earlier stages of my career, when I functioned largely on my own and then in charge of teams in a management capacity. The shift from being a solo manager leading a team to a manager of a larger operation is minor when compared to the monumental shift of managing an operation *and* being part of an executive team. That next level—when you're working on an executive team with colleagues—can present an entirely different set of challenges and require a new set of skills. I know I certainly needed coaching.

You may find that the most efficient way to unify the team is to bring in a leadership coach to work with the team as a group. Adding skill sets isn't easy, no matter where you are. You may need help to let go of the desire to control all the elements of any major initiative. Making a constant effort to surround yourself with talent and working at improving yourself and others in the process are key.

One way to gauge your own ability as a leader is to ask your team to give you answers to the following questions on a periodic basis:

1. What do I do particularly well that I should do more of and build on?
2. What do I do poorly that is hurting the team and requires my attention and commitment to change?

3. How could I do better? What actions would help me improve and improve our team performance?
4. What do I spend my time on that I need to do more of?
5. What do I spend time and energy on that I need to do less of, delegate to someone else, or stop all together?
6. How else could I improve my performance and that of our team?

Be certain your team knows that you'll treat their answers as constructive and strictly anonymous. With that understanding, you may receive some surprising answers. Be sure to take the critical step of having a session with the team in which you review the feedback and let them know what you plan to do to respond to their suggestions. You have asked for help and your credibility will rest on the humility, candor, and follow through you demonstrate in your response.

If reading your team's input is difficult, take particular care with preparing yourself for this meeting. The more difficult the feedback, the more important that you respond in a way that demonstrates genuine desire to improve and gratitude for the team members' honesty. How you initiate the conversation, how you express yourself, how you frame any follow-up questions of your own or from your team, even how you carry yourself: every detail speaks volumes. If you have a leadership coach or other outside resource, talk through the meeting in advance, in detail. Understand that this follow-up meeting is an opportunity to improve yourself, recognize and model the value of candor, and build trust. The grace with which you handle this conversation is crucial for you and for the team.

Building Trust

For anyone who is or aspires to be a leader, I recommend Patrick Lencioni's best-selling book *Five Dysfunctions of a Team: A Leadership Fable*. Lencioni suggests there are five major dysfunctions that threaten to destroy any team. He presents these dysfunctions as a sort of cascade, beginning with absence of trust, which fuels further dysfunctions so that eventually the team and its mission are in shambles. Absence of trust is the source of a lot of team dysfunction in general and establishing trust must start when a team is first formed.

The first time I went to an executive off-site where we were asked to talk about ourselves, our life story, our passions, our hopes and dreams, I was skeptical and impatient, possibly visibly so on both counts. I expected that most hard-driving executives also viewed this kind of stuff as a giant waste of time. I was wrong. As it turned out, many of my presumptions about other people were off the mark, sometimes even by 180 degrees.

Getting people together and encouraging them to talk about themselves can in fact be a great trust builder—when done well. The leader's job hinges upon enabling people to understand each other, to understand their motivations and their character. Your team members reveal themselves when they speak. They explain where they're coming from and discuss the experiences that have shaped them. Trust and cooperation can grow. On the flip side, some people use sharing opportunities to tell self-aggrandizing stories that actually foster resentment. It's important to shape and drive these situations to make sure that the stories bring people together, rather than create walls between them. Since not every executive has the skills to lead this discussion, investing in an experienced facilitator can be very worthwhile.

Time spent building the team, working on team dynamics, and learning why this specific initiative is worthy of our time and energy is key. The trust we need to drive change comes from understanding people's motivations, the *why* behind what we do. Without that insight, people can too often ascribe actions to the wrong motivation and thus resist change. Spending time together enables that understanding and rapport to develop. Lencioni's book and others offer valuable suggestions on team building. The critical point is that team-building efforts are an important investment and part of the process of building trust.

Facing Conflict

It's not easy to face conflicts without first establishing trust. Trust is more than a feeling of security or an absence of fear. Trust enables assured reliance on the character, ability, strength, and truth of others. If you do not establish trust—both between yourself and your team and among individual team members—a fear of conflict will dominate team members' interactions. Recognize that trust and fear are especially closely linked and that fear stunts dialogue and discussion. To have real dialogues that get at real concerns, team members have to be willing to confront one another and resolve any conflicts. Your job as a leader is to create an environment where people feel safe doing so without fearing personal reprisals or punishment. People need time together and shared experiences for trust to grow, to become comfortable with others' motivations, character, and intent. If you don't create that safe environment, you'll wind up with a team full of people going out of their way to avoid potential conflicts, people who are more interested in not rocking the boat than in fully exploring potential problems.

Beyond the basics of treating everyone with respect, empathy, and consideration, there's no one prescribed way to create a safe environment for dialogue; corporate cultures vary. In some places, you may find a very lively, almost combative culture of debate; in others, politeness is highly valued. Of course, there are cultural differences to think of as well. The issues of fear and conflict and how to deal with them are fundamentally different in an American corporation versus a Chinese corporation, for example. As with all the issues ahead of you, you have to devise the solution to fit the context. Once you have established a foundation of trust and constructive conflict, resistance decreases and the process moves more smoothly.

Focusing the Leadership Team

You cannot achieve team unity overnight. We don't have one meeting or one team-building retreat and then pledge our undying commitment to one another and to the change. But we can begin the process and urge people toward a place where they understand debate and discussion not as personal attacks but as a vital part of working through issues and refining the change. In doing so, we will also combine our efforts into focusing on commitment, accountability, and results to ensure the long-range success of the change.

The notion that a team gets better simply by working together is not necessarily true. Just as with leadership, practice can't get you there unless you're practicing the right skills and at the appropriate level. Practicing the wrong skills with the wrong dynamics can lead straight to a dead end. Changing behavior is difficult; without compelling actionable feedback, it is virtually impossible. Team leaders are wise to drive continuous improvement of themselves and their teams by measuring and assessing their team dynamics using a variety of methods.

~~~~~

You need to assemble, build, and strengthen the leadership team, all while offering clarity about what you've been convened to do. One function the team is not charged with is making the final decisions. A team exists to perfect the change, and even the best of teams still requires you to take point on the major decisions. A mentor's simple phrase still rings in my head: "a voice is not a vote." A voice is an opportunity to raise objections and make suggestions. It is not a vote, and a leadership team is not a democracy. This is where the idea of commitment comes in. As leader, you must be able to stand behind each decision you make and consistently carry out the plan you've all developed. The commitment starts at the top with you and then spreads out through the rest of the team.

You do have the final say, and that should be clear to your team members. And the more these individuals contribute to a plan, the more personally invested they become. This is where accountability comes in. If a team develops a plan for change and commits to carrying it out, ideally all members have a stake in it. Cultivating a sense of ownership in the debate process can increase each person's sense of responsibility for resultant decisions. And in the long term, that encourages attention to the results.

With your leadership team assembled and unified, you are ready for the hard work ahead. We've established the need and urgency for change in Step One and begun assembling and unifying the leadership team in Step Two. We now need to craft our compelling vision of the future, the subject of Step Three.

Developing and Communicating a Clear and Compelling Vision of the Future

ONCE YOU HAVE YOUR leadership team in place, you and your team must be ready to envision and communicate the future in such a vivid and irresistible way that everyone understands your vision and appreciates your passion for it. By now, you're convinced of the need for this innovative change. But convincing others can be much more difficult and time consuming than you might first anticipate. Leading change has often been compared to preparing for and leading an expedition, and with good reason. As the leader, you must ensure that everyone can work together with the same goal in sight.

And "everyone" is not just the leadership team, but everyone around you. You won't accomplish this step in a conversation or two. You have to deliver a carefully crafted message to every group of stakeholders, a message with a central core as well as add-ons adapted for each unique audience. Your technology team will require a different emphasis from that of operations, which will be different from that of frontline sales, marketing, human resources, and every other group of stakeholders. Perhaps you'll spend one morning explaining to one group of people how your vision of the future will increase profits, and the same afternoon telling another group how the proposed change will kick start operational efficiency or improve customer service. Each time you explain your vision is an important message to others and a useful process for you. By emphasizing different parts of your vision to different people, you can develop a more precise, more holistic picture of your proposed changes. All of your messages become part of your vision for a better, more successful future.

These concepts may seem very similar to those of Step One, establishing a need to change, and in some aspects, they are. Both of these steps are fundamentally about creating or revealing dissatisfaction with the way things are today. However, in the earlier step, we were simply attempting to convince others that *the status quo is unacceptable* and the way we are doing things today no longer works; we need to do something different as we move into the future. In Step Three, we develop and present a very *specific idea* of what that "something different" is. In most cases, this means comparing the present to a future that is very different. The challenges are to inspire people—many of whom have been comfortable where they are—and to get them excited and involved enough that they want to head into that future, that they become eager to participate in this expedition to the new.

Up until this point in rolling out your change, only a few people in the organization have heard your presentation on the need for urgent change. They're the ones with the authority to approve your initiative and those you've recruited to help you craft a vision for the future. After all, you can't go around the company telling layers of management and employees that prospects are dreadful, horrible threats loom, and change is urgently needed—but you don't yet know what that change is, let alone how to implement it. To do so would create all kinds of chaos. Instead, you've talked about the need for change with a relatively small circle, many of whom will partner with you and own the task of crafting a bold vision of the future and the plan to get there.

Leaving the Status Quo and Creating the Future

Whether you are bringing change to an existing organization or developing a start-up, you must give people a clear—and strongly compelling—vision of the future: where the organization is going and their role in the new future. If your stakeholders are deeply invested in maintaining the status quo, you will certainly encounter resistance. You must do more than just prepare for that resistance. You must understand it and the reasons that people feel it. While you've been imagining the future and perhaps engaging in "blue-sky thinking," they've been focused on what they believe works.

Momentum is critical in the early steps of transformative change. To begin building that momentum, you first must start communicating the vision to everyone in your company. You must make your commitment to the vision of the future—the change you are driving—real to your people and do everything possible to get everyone in the same state of mind. But no matter how energetic and enthusiastic you may be, you can't do this alone. You must be sure the entire leadership team is—and stays—fully on board so that they too are actively creating this future. Prepare yourself to spend a lot of time gathering facts, debating options, and clarifying the vision.

Back in 1995 as internet trading was just emerging, we had developed a strategy to have two divisions of Schwab offer online trading at different price points. The online-only service was branded as e.Schwab, with limited service and rock-bottom pricing; the Charles Schwab online/offline hybrid service had a higher price point. This combination enabled us to compete with e.Trade and others, but customers were confused and growing dissatisfied over time.

It was clear that the industry was changing and we needed to as well, but this wasn't obvious and immediate to everyone in the company. To the outside world, our numbers looked good, so we didn't have a clear "burning platform" to urge people to adopt the change. We were enormously profitable at the time, and to simplify and offer Schwab service with e.Schwab pricing would require us to take a big financial hit, at least in the short term. But as it stood, the tiered pricing system of online brokerage was not customer-oriented and was a fundamental violation of Schwab's corporate culture, which encouraged us to always do the right thing for the customer.

How then to create a sense of urgency around this change and unite people, when we could have put it off until later? We had done the projections and knew that without the pricing change, our lead in the marketplace would soon evaporate. But numbers don't necessarily persuade and excite people. We had to conjure two different visions of the future. To convince the team that Schwab's position wasn't as secure as some might think, I reached out to four of the disgruntled customers who had written me letters detailing their frustrations with the tiered internet pricing system then in place. I asked them to meet with our leadership team and tell them about these grievances.

With each of these high-revenue customers right in front of them, describing in detail how they felt the company was doing them a disservice and eroding their trust in the process, the problem became hard to ignore. These long-standing, high-caliber customers felt that the company was not meeting their needs and was instead violating the implied customer contract. Conveying this information directly to the team was a critical part of establishing an urgent need to change. These stories, delivered in person and with great passion, were far more persuasive than any tidy columns of numbers on a spreadsheet might have been.

We began to realize that by acting quickly and decisively, we could halt this tide of customer dissatisfaction and reestablish ourselves as the responsive, customer-first company we had always been. Even if we did experience a temporary revenue or profit slump with this change, our market share leadership of trades and accounts would actually skyrocket. Since the internet brokerage ecosystem was growing rapidly and becoming intensely more competitive daily, we knew we had to act. Just as we had predicted, the stock value went down promptly after we made the change, plummeting nearly 50 percent in days. We had anticipated this and were even prepared to weather a few years of poor stock performance. We had been honest with our board, analysts, and investors about this aspect of the change, never glossing over the risks. Everyone knew the change was going to seriously lower our profits for a time.

And then, also as we had predicted, the customers stopped trickling away. They began trading more and more often. By quickly adapting to fulfill customer desires, we had distinguished ourselves, reinforced our customer-first reputation, and positioned ourselves for a huge wave of volume growth eventually followed by a wave of revenue and profit growth as well. Prospective new customers began to show interest in the new pricing scheme. We recovered faster than even our most hopeful projections had suggested. Our stock climbed back to its pre-change value—and then doubled in worth by the end of the year. That same year, our stock valuation passed that of Merrill Lynch. In twelve months, we had gone from a crazy company tossing away our lead in the market to a bunch of geniuses who had done an end run around disaster.

We couldn't have gotten there without first strengthening the leadership team. As it turned out, facing the facts and debating the alternatives was an extremely healthy team-building activity for our leadership. At the beginning, not everyone was convinced this change was necessary. But as we dug into our customer metrics, explored our trends, and analyzed financial projections of how the change process would unfold, the team gelled around the need and we all came to own the vision for where we were going: one Charles Schwab with a highly competitive pricing structure for our online trades. Our depth of understanding and our combined passion about the need for the change enabled us to sell the need for a pricing change to the next layer of leadership, to the hundreds of managers who ran all parts of the company, and ultimately to all 11,500 employees. It soon was very clear to all of us—those who carried the message and those who heard it—that this change was urgent, necessary, and connected to the mission of our company, and would lead to an exciting future for Charles Schwab.

Showing Your Passion

Whether it's creating a start-up or a new pricing structure, you have to believe in the change passionately—and share that passion over the long haul. In a sense, you have to invent the future. You have to imagine what could be—and what has to happen to get there. And you have to genuinely believe in what you are envisioning. People won't follow leaders who *say* all the right things but don't *act* according to what they claim to believe. They want to see their leaders making personal commitments and taking personal risks. Leaders have to be willing to publicly stake their reputations on the ideas they are advocating.

Passion is something that you can't teach and that you have to keep in full supply. Change requires a lot of energy and a lot of repetition. Leaders must spread the message to different groups and multiple times to the same group, in different ways and in various situations. This repetition can be frustrating and tax your patience. But frustration and impatience will not help bring the change about.

No matter how many times or in how many venues you've described the change and the need, you have to be consistent. Keep at it and do whatever it takes to enable people to understand, in real terms, what the change entails. Your immediate goal must be to get them to the point that they understand the change and see the vision of the future—and they know they can get there.

~~~~~

There are two consistently recurring themes in presenting a compelling vision:

1. The critical need to communicate a compelling vision of the future—and to patiently communicate that message over and over
2. The importance of balancing enthusiasm and passion about the need for change with compassion, empathy, and understanding about the effort the change process requires

In this step, we have discussed *what* you need to communicate to the organization. The *how* of that communication effort, you've read about in Chapters Three and Four of Part One, so you know that your ability to lead change rests on your character and skills as a communicator. Developing yourself in these areas is an immersive process, as deep as it is rewarding. Communication is critical throughout the entire process; it is vital to each of the steps for *Driving Disruption* and transcends all of them. Make developing and improving your communication skills a priority, always. Those skills are essential, for communicating the vision behind the change effort is never over; it's something you must repeat and constantly reinforce.

Practice empathy and develop your listening skills to fully understand how others may see this change and its impact on them. Allow your empathy and your humanity to come through and your communication will be that much more effective. Further, a healthy dose of curiosity is invaluable, both to be open to the new and to continue learning at every opportunity. With that outlook, you may see that any opposition or resistance you encounter can also reveal the problems you'll have to solve. Recognizing the issues early gives you a huge advantage. What to do when you spot them is the subject of Step Four.

Planning Ahead for Known and Unknown Barriers

EVERY PROJECT COMES WITH a host of potential barriers to success. Part of developing a solid plan for implementation involves thinking through these roadblocks before you encounter them. The fourth step in the *Driving Disruption* process is all about anticipating problems as you are planning—and confronting these problems before they derail your efforts. You might well wonder if this isn't simply a piece of the planning process (Step Five). The answer is not a simple yes or no; it's more involved.

The planning process will require a team of highly engaged people, a team that may begin to extend beyond the inner team discussed in Step Two. It will also require time to develop the fully built-out design for a bold, breakthrough change. If you haven't considered and dealt with the most obvious and potentially difficult barriers at the earliest stages of the project, your initiative can be undermined and derailed before it has even left the station.

Ideally you will think through potential problems as an extension of your original vision. Innovative change typically originates when we observe trends and realize that something has to be done differently. We have to extend the reach of that critical thinking to consider the possible effects of the change we are proposing. Unfortunately, no one can anticipate every problem. In general, however, the early or initial difficulties you will encounter when introducing these changes fall into four broad categories. So many great change initiatives are given up for lost or destroyed because of these difficulties that I refer to them as the "Bermuda Quadrangle"—a tongue-in-cheek reference to the Bermuda Triangle, the area in the western part of the North Atlantic roughly between Florida, Bermuda, and Puerto Rico known for unexplained disappearances of ships, planes, and people.

Mapping the Bermuda Quadrangle

Given the emotional, social, and psychological issues that leaders must address in all steps of the change process, it should come as no surprise that people issues underlie all points of the Bermuda Quadrangle. Just as some of the dangers in the Bermuda Triangle stem from the shallow shoals that lie beneath the surface, the issues that compose the Bermuda Quadrangle—resistance, skills, processes, and company culture—are not always clearly marked or identified. But they exist, to varying degrees. Further, the danger represented by each point of the quadrangle can shift, becoming stronger and more significant without warning. Be aware and on the lookout for these issues as you plan and then execute the changes you propose.

People Resist Change

What will people resist? What will they embrace? What can you do to allay people's fears about the change and get them on board? What leaders see as a promising path to the future, others may perceive as overwhelmingly dangerous leaps. Leaders must prepare people for the journey ahead; getting it right demands the empathy and patience to see others' concerns and points of view. I've been teaching these ideas for years—yet sometimes I need reminders.

Before the first day of class in the Fall 2013 Wharton Executive MBA program, I had thought through a change for my elective course on leading breakthrough change. By the time they get to this course, the students—emerging leaders who fit in classes while dealing with real problems in their jobs—have had their fill of case studies. Instead, I had a new, exciting plan for the final assignment that seemed like a win on all levels. In teams of five to six, students would explore relevant data and develop concepts and implementation plans to solve a real-world problem; they would then present their ideas to a panel of the school's administrators, who were eager for input. Students would have free rein in their proposals and would get valuable experience in developing, presenting, and defending their ideas—challenges that mirrored what they would face back at work. I sensed some discomfort in class, but trusted that the students would rise to the task. What I didn't know then was just how unnerving this change was to many of them.

Soon enough, I learned that a number of students were actively considering dropping the class on the basis of this change to the final project. Then it hit me: I was so enthused about the project's learning potential that I hadn't taken the time to consider the *students'* perspectives or to explain the *purpose* behind the change. So, I returned to my principles of leading breakthrough change, focused on the problem to be solved, and considered how I might bring the students with me. In opening the next session, I explained that I had skipped over crucial steps and missed the opportunity to thoroughly describe the purpose of the change and the benefits I envisioned. I made clear that I was interested in hearing any and all concerns about the final project. After hearing my more thorough explanation and discussing their concerns, the class could decide, via anonymous vote, whether to stay with the new approach or reinstate the project as it had been in previous years.

As it turned out, the initial concern that some class members had voiced—of having already mentally prepared themselves for the initial project—was just the first layer, not the real issue. Deeper into the discussion, they voiced apprehensions that more closely reflected how people often see change as a threat. Students were worried about offending the administration and putting themselves on the line with ideas that might be unconventional, groundbreaking, or untried. They were anxious that the new project would take more time, energy, and creativity and that grading would be hard. These are all valid concerns and, as they came to see, ones that leaders must face and overcome when aiming for anything greater than incremental change.

After this animated class, the vote was nearly unanimous for the new project. The teams took it on enthusiastically and found it a challenging and immediately useful learning experience. They developed an appreciation for how long it can take to inspire others to embrace a new, innovative idea and how critical it is to think through and thoroughly describe the practical details for implementation. I wish I could say it was all planned, but my initial gaffe of inadequately introducing the change turned out to be a useful part of the students' learning process—and such a powerful reminder that I still relate this story to underscore the importance of engaging others, understanding perspectives, and clarifying the benefits of change.

Resistance comes in many forms and can be well hidden in any venue—and particularly in the workplace. In many cases, employees fall into one of three groups. A small group, say 5 percent, will readily embrace the change; perhaps 15 percent never will. Those who are in the middle can make the change and may need some help to do so. If you get the 5 percent focused on creating the proof of concept pilot and leading the way with their energy, vision, and passion, they can bring the 80 percent along quickly. The hitch is that you have to identify and replace those who can't make the changes before they drag the group down. You have to get everyone on board. Without that, you simply can't get a realistic assessment of what it's going to take to get the change propagated across the organization—and you certainly can't get there with any speed.

Skills Are Missing

You have to be sure you have the people you need in order to implement the changes—and that they have (or can readily acquire) the new skills and new perspective the change demands. A great attitude is required but is not sufficient. Part of your advance planning must be a careful assessment of what skills will be needed, how they can be developed in-house, and where you can find them outside. A few thoughts to consider:

- What array of skills will this project demand?
- Do we currently have enough people with the specific, targeted skills and experiences to successfully implement the changes and complete this project?
- If the answer to the previous question is no, how much time do we have before we need to be fully staffed? Will the organization tolerate the time required to train current employees or recruit new people?
- If the necessary skills don't currently exist in the organization, how soon can we find people with the necessary skills

and experience to bring believability to the idea that the project can succeed?

- How and where can we find the necessary support people?
- If the company has previously hired for a totally different skill set, what other strategies can we use?

You'll have to find ways to get people to adapt, or else actively recruit new people. Most likely you'll do both. The most difficult piece of this equation is making a realistic assessment of whether the people you have either possess or can learn the skills necessary to get where you need to go. If the answer is no—and it often is—then you'll likely have the wrenching task of cutting staff who have been with you for a long while to make room for the new people. One of the more unfortunate realities of leading change is that not everyone can follow you. But if you've been attending to your network and developing yourself as a magnet for talent, finding people with the right skills will not be a huge barrier.

Processes Are Rigid

Next is the problem of overly rigid processes and procedures. If you are proposing a change to established processes and procedures, you may be up against years of institutional habits and mind-sets. So you must determine where the company is set in its ways and decide what it will take to change those procedures and mind-sets. Don't underestimate the challenge this presents— and be sure that those above you, your boss or maybe the board, understand and support the change you are proposing.

Bear in mind that organizations are built and structured for reliability, consistency, predictability, and control. Their processes and procedures have been designed to deliver these results. Many employees' self-image and perception of their personal worth are rooted in their knowledge of these processes and reinforced by their own heartfelt belief in the processes' critical importance to the company.

But disruptive change stirs up everything. It isn't reliable, consistent, or predictable. The new procedures put in place to deal with the current reality may be immature and not yet up to the task. And that is only the beginning. The changes themselves will often challenge the fundamental necessity or even the relevance of long-trusted processes, which are typically rather inflexible.

Chances are that over time, every long-standing process will undergo scrutiny and will change to some degree. Think of how you deliver and measure customer service, measure advertising, develop and test technology, schedule and administer meetings, identify high performers, design employee benefits, and measure morale. In all these and more, flexibility and adaptability become ever more important.

Company Culture Is Unyielding

The decision that your boss or board makes is heavily influenced by the final category of risk marking the Bermuda Quadrangle: corporate culture. Think about the change you're proposing in the context of the entire enterprise. Does this change fit in with the values of the existing corporate culture? If it does, how can you best make that connection clear? If it doesn't, or even if it's simply *perceived* as violating a corporate cultural value, you will likely face ongoing resistance.

Sometimes the difference lies in the questions you ask. Consider the difference between asking, "Does the initiative fit or not fit our culture and our values?" versus framing the question as "Can we connect this initiative to our culture and values so that it is a new expression of those values rather than something that's in conflict with them?"

If the change is so dramatic that it cannot be made to fit within the existing corporate cultural values, then you must prepare for a long uphill battle. Those employees who are most threatened by the project will use this conflict with values and traditions as a lever to undermine your leadership and drive a stake into the project's legitimate fit in the company. You can overcome this, but doing so will take a lot of time and effort and will be a huge distraction. Better to find a way to make the project fit the culture and its values; by avoiding the problem, you can create more momentum for the initiative.

Compounding the Dangers

As if navigating the Bermuda Quadrangle weren't already difficult enough, the problems represented in the four points of the quadrangle are rarely so distinct. Often, they can't be compartmentalized into one of these four barriers. For example, a people problem can also be a skill problem as well as a corporate culture problem; a processes problem can also be a culture problem.

Difficulties often stem from resistance and an entrenched company culture. That combination can render even smart, capable operators surprisingly ineffective.

Find the change agents inside the culture. Identify people who block change as well. You may need to bring in people from the outside who have no history with the company and can take on change more aggressively, with less personal baggage. This is a lesson we faced at Schwab in instituting the changes to the branch network. When we began to transition to proactive customer development, we had not yet developed and nurtured the skills that employees would need for the additional outbound calls and interactions with customers they would be undertaking. This skill gap was so large that over the course of five years, approximately 80 percent of the branch employees were unable to make the transition to our new model of service. At this point, I had neither the experience nor the skills to make this change less disruptive and more successful. Instead, it hurled us through all points of the Bermuda Quadrangle in what felt like slow motion; it was our own perfect storm. We all learned from it—and came to better appreciate the importance of advance planning and anticipating barriers.

If you and your leadership team have actively expanded your networks and become talent magnets (see Chapter Two), you are much better placed to face even compounded dangers and recruit the people you need, when you need them the most.

Planning for the Unexpected

When you are navigating the Bermuda Quadrangle, you need an advance plan and flexibility, since you are bound to come upon barriers and issues unexpectedly. A good plan is all about anticipation. You have to look not just at current issues but at ones that may crop up only after the change goes into effect.

The way to prepare for the unexpected is to explicitly talk it out, and not just inside your head. Gather executives, responsible business partners, and any other people whose involvement is critical to the change you propose and ask them all to think seriously about how the change might be received within the organization and outside of the organization, and what could go wrong. In developing the ideas for your change, as you broaden your reach and expand your net, be sure to get more perspectives as early as possible to better appreciate what the initial reactions might be.

Once you are excited about the vision and are completely convinced that it's worthy of time, energy, and passion, it can be hard to take a step back to fully appreciate how others might see it from a wholly different point of view. By bringing others into the process of discovery and imagination, together you can be more realistic about how people will view the change and how you can best present the ideas.

Uncover and Examine Potential Resistance

Leaders must anticipate resistance and even look for specific issues of resistance in advance. Early on, the leadership team should be making comprehensive lists of the ways employees are going to push back; determining the time, assets, and staff you'll need to make the plan work; and carefully considering the ways the change will—or might seem to—conflict with the corporate culture as it stands.

Take the time to explore and think in detail about the risks and the uncertainties ahead so that you can eventually manage them proactively and create comprehensive ways to defuse these issues. While it's tempting to lump risks and uncertainties together (and perhaps underestimate both as a consequence), be careful to tease out the differences. Risks are measurable: you may not be able to predict with certainty exactly what will happen, but you can make a reasonable estimate of the odds of success versus the odds of the project going wrong. In contrast, uncertainties are both unknown and unknowable: these appear on the horizon with no warning and require that you adapt and adjust in the moment.

When we were preparing to implement the internet pricing change at Schwab, we were committed to identifying all the risks and potential issues we possibly could. So, we held a meeting with our top two layers of management. We broke the group up into teams of ten or so and asked them to imagine that they were having a meeting with the next layer of executives. Where did they expect to see pushback and resistance to the projects? What could they identify as roadblocks? What questions might they be asked? What further information might that next layer of executives need?

In addition to having them anticipate that next level of rollout, we were hoping to learn what objections and fears they held, fears they might not fully or frankly voice on their own behalf.

We made it clear that we were there to listen and learn, with completely open minds.

This approach of coming to the conversation curious requires a level of openness and engagement that may be new for some leaders. When you're ready to sell, persuade, and convince, it can be very hard to hear responses and questions that make you uncomfortable or that seem to undermine the approach you've taken. But those critiques, questions, and issues are part of the workplace. Refusing to acknowledge them doesn't make them disappear; in fact, avoiding them undermines your credibility as a leader.

Anticipating people's specific resistance requires you to put yourself in their shoes. Problems surprise us because we are coming at situations from our perspective without taking into account the perspectives that others may have. As my Wharton students reminded me, what might seem a minor shift to you may well be a huge issue that others will lose sleep over. Getting your top people together and creating an open forum is a great way to get inside their heads in a nonthreatening atmosphere. Individuals may not have been comfortable raising these issues one-on-one for fear of being alone in their fears or objections. Ask for theoretical objections and questions. The concerns that surface help provide a broader and more in-depth understanding of people's perspectives. Get them out in the open and you can begin to resolve them.

Tempting as it may be to skip or rush through this step en route to the change you're driving, if you miss this opportunity or fail to present it in a way that makes it real and allows for honest feedback, the gap in understanding could have dire consequences for the overall success of your change initiative. And even if you do gather and incorporate feedback into the overall plan, consider that there may still be issues that haven't been uncovered. People may simply be too enmeshed in the history or the culture to have the perspective they really need. In some circumstances, you may need an entirely new perspective, from outside.

Outside Experts Can Sharpen the Focus

Using outsiders can help you better anticipate the barriers you will face or even see the opportunities that are already in front of you. After almost four years of mediocre efforts at downsizing at Schwab, we finally made the decision to bring in consultants.

They immediately saw hundreds of millions of dollars of potential cost savings that we had missed. Similarly, when Intel faced the need to downsize from 2005 to 2007, what had to be done was also a difficult cultural fit. Intel's CEO and CFO ultimately brought in the same consultants Schwab had used, and the company managed to save billions. Intel's CFO later credited the success of this effort to the perspective we gained from our consulting team, and these consultants ended up working with us for almost a decade on a broad host of assignments. We learned we could benefit greatly from advisors who had exceptional experiences that were outside of our own. These included embedding a philosophy of continuous rightsizing of corporate functions, improved processes around acquisition analytics and post-deal assessments, new ways of thinking about capital structure, and the rational deployment of debt.

In my experiences and those of my interviewees, outside consultants play a huge role in the success of bold, innovative change. They are valuable repositories of new experiences, new wisdom, and challenging perspectives—including the critical perspective that can debunk corporate mythologies.

~~~~~

Step Four addresses significant issues you may face in developing and implementing plans for change. Keeping the dangers represented in the Bermuda Quadrangle in mind, ask yourself, "What resistance, gaps in skill sets, problems in processes, and cultural issues are likely to arise if we install the new, transformative change we decided on in Step Three?"

When you are leading change, human nature, market conditions, and inertia work against you. The best way to resolve this is to take the time, in advance, to think through what problems are likely to arise. If you look down the road, you can develop a plan that either prevents those issues from becoming true problems or responds to them so effectively that they won't fester into something worse or gather momentum across the organization. That part of the planning process is the focus of Step Five.

Creating and Managing a Workable Plan

WITH STEP FIVE, WE move beyond establishing the groundwork for creating a new future and get down to the nitty-gritty of planning the details of disruptive change. By now you have a clear idea of the impact your change will have and a sense of the problems and barriers you may face in implementing it. By definition, bold change initiatives fly in the face of the indicators that organizations like. Plus they introduce entirely new risks. Sometimes lots of them. How then can you realistically estimate results or timing? The short answer is you must dramatically modify and rethink some basic processes since truly innovative change demands something different.

Making Assessments: From the Present to the Future

Starting anew with blue-sky thinking and long-term planning have certain parallels: the need to assess where you are, where you want to be, and how to get there. These assessments are vital to leading disruptive change, whether you are starting from scratch, reshaping an aspect of the business, entering on a new market, or looking to expand your reach.

Initial Assessment: Where We Are

Whatever the business and circumstances, virtually all plans begin with a thorough assessment of "where we are" (WWA). This assessment should take into account not just operations and processes, but all other factors that contribute to an organization's position in the marketplace. You want to look at competitive position, customer satisfaction and quality of output, productivity and efficiency, human resource considerations, and other factors. Any or all of these aspects may need to change in order to get your vision off the ground.

You must also gauge all the skills your team will need over the course of the initiative: marketing, sales, operational efficiency, familiarity with social networking, and whatever else your specific change initiative requires. Do you have those skills on your team? If not, where can you get them? Whether it's consulting firms, staffing agencies, online recruiting sources, or simply going to other departments within the company, have a plan to get the expertise you require.

An inexperienced or overconfident leader can make a misstep in many junctures. In the early planning stage, for example, many managers project the current state of affairs into the future, including some marginal improvements in productivity and quality. Simple, linear projections are fine if you are planning for incremental change. In fact, this is a predictable, reliable, low-risk approach that may be the right course of action. If, however, you are aiming for transformative change, you will need to do much more.

Assessment for Disruptive Change: Where We Want to Be

Truly innovative, disruptive change demands a leap to a fundamentally new and different position. Assuming that's the kind of change we're after, the second big assessment revolves around "where we want to be" (WWWTB). Whether from habit, education, or a desire to take the safe course, leaders often define WWWTB as a simple projection of WWA, perhaps with modest or even aggressive improvement. But truly innovative change is not incremental; it's a chance to substantially redefine the future to be something very new and different, a competitive leap forward. You don't want people to picture just more of the same, only faster; nor do you want them to define the future by what you're doing today. As the driver of disruptive change, it's your job to expand the conversation from the start and, building on what you began in Step Three, fully articulate your concept of the future with clear, more specifically developed and measurable goals.

The conversations you want to encourage—creative, wonderfully energizing discussions of the range of possibilities—become the new starting point in contemplating WWWTB. These are true dialogues, open-ended, multidirectional conversations in which you and your people are imagining the most timely, highest-potential changes. At this stage, you want to think imaginatively, envisioning the galaxy of a different future. Change, particularly disruptive change, is a process of exploration and discovery along the way. When it's time to make choices, you want to be able to choose from a wide array of possibilities.

It is far easier and more productive to discuss weaknesses and strengths of the project at the outset than once it's under way. So be sure to build in the space to learn and the flexibility to redefine the destination—all without the economics completely falling apart. If you don't carefully consider the terms and resource needs until you're further down the road or if you overcommit, your request for more time or money may be seen as a sign that you are slipping or missing commitments. Much better to negotiate early, ensuring your resources are adequate and with some contingencies built in for the unknowns that will inevitably pop up during this leap toward the future.

Assessment for Action: How Do We Get There?

The first two assessments lead logically to the third: "how do we get there?" (HDWGT). That is, how do we get from WWA to WWWTB? The second assessment, WWWTB, is the vision question that we first discussed in Step Three. The difference is that rather than painting a broad-brush, sweeping picture of the future, here we must define that future as a set of specific goals, deliverables, and metrics, because now we are creating the actual plan. When you can fully answer the *how*, breaking it down in terms of partitioning, metrics, people, and pilots (Steps Six and Seven), then you will have developed a meaningful plan of action. This stage in breakthrough change requires an even greater recognition of the unforeseen than the usual planning process for incremental change. Because your pathway to the future is not continuous or predictable, be sure to leave room in the plan for missteps, dead ends, delays, and a great deal of learning along the way.

Getting a group from where you are to where you want to be requires that you create a bridge enabling your people to see where you are leading them—and to put their trust in you and the project. That is exactly why you must consider, carefully and thoroughly, each of the questions inherent in the three assessments.

Planning Components

Like many other business plans, the plan for a breakthrough change has the key components of goals and deliverables, tasks, deadlines, capital and other resources, and people—and you'll often need to deal with these components differently. You can't know exactly what the outcome will be at the beginning of an innovative change initiative, but if you use the steps, you will have a reasonably good idea.

Goals and Deliverables

You will need to define specific sets of executable goals and deliverables multiple times over the life of the initiative. You can usually partition breakthrough change into a number of discrete initiatives with defined deliverables. By dividing your overall goal into smaller, step-by-step goals, you will have a series of checkpoints that you can use to determine if you are on track. By subdividing a single, giant goal into smaller targets, you allow for more control and opportunities to build momentum.

Breaking down the initiative into a series of goals is also a useful way to deal with potential shortages of time and money. If resources and time frames are tight, scaling down the deliverable definition may be a solution. For example, this could involve an initial launch in a limited number of locations rather than a complete rollout. Your new deliverable becomes that first small pilot implementation, and you will reevaluate the overall plan after that portion is completed. (A detailed discussion of pilot implementations is in Step Seven.)

Tasks

Once you have the broad strokes of a plan, you must lay out the tasks you need to accomplish. This part of the planning process remains the same for most project and operational plans, whether the change is incremental or bold and disruptive. Pushback and resistance are nearly inevitable with most changes—and they will cause delays and cost money. You must anticipate and plan for this, to avoid or at least minimize disappointments and difficult conversations with your superiors if you miss deadlines or struggle to hit your budgets.

Deadlines

Deadlines are incredibly important in projects of this nature. You must constantly reinforce the importance of critical deadlines as they relate to key deliverables. Breakthrough initiatives often have many moving parts that are interrelated. Pause or remove one and everything grinds to a halt. A single delay along a critical path will push everything back. Delays are the enemy of ambitious initiatives, for they eat away at resources, team credibility, and momentum. You combat delay the same way leaders approach other problems: anticipate, anticipate, anticipate. Build an expectation of delays into your plan and don't cut time frames too close to the bone.

You must build the sense that every key deadline will somehow be met. It may require weekends and late nights, but the team must—and will—rise to the occasion. Without this attitude, practice, and commitment, slippage will pile upon slippage. A few small lapses can seem innocent on their own, but if they build on one another they can derail your whole initiative. You must develop an ambitious (and realistic) plan and guide the team toward the goals. In the process, be sure to continually build and maintain commitment and a spirit of determination.

Capital and Other Resources

In examining the gap between where we are and where we want to be, leaders will begin to identify the resources necessary to get there. There's likely to be a series of economic and institutional limits on those resources. As a result, the budgets typically awarded for these projects seem much tighter to those who are responsible for the actual outcomes. You need to negotiate from a place of strength and knowledge to secure the best possible framework for your change initiative. It is far wiser to negotiate your needs up front, even before signing on, so you can discuss weaknesses and strengths of the project without having them reflect on you.

The process of putting limits—putting gates—on funding provides a reality check and time for reevaluation. It allows you to explore big ideas without committing big money. It puts a check on leaders who may allow their enthusiasm for a project's vision to result in underestimating potential difficulties and challenges. It is all too easy to imagine that a project will be less difficult and less expensive than it really will be, that the capital and other resources we've been allotted will be more than enough to complete the project. Why? Change often seems "simple," perhaps even obvious—even when it is neither.

While I've learned just how hard change can be, I persist as a change junkie. The question that rings in my head is often "How hard can it be?" Addressing that very question with honesty and depth is difficult and critical. This tendency to underestimate applies to time and resource requirements (such as money and personnel). Given the unpredictability of bold change initiatives, budgetary overruns do not necessarily mean the project is failing. Instead, if planning is thorough and information is shared early, problems that might otherwise seem disastrous can be overcome.

An honest projection, clearly communicated, can be powerful. Particularly in a bleak financial atmosphere, the temptation may be to present a rosier picture, or even simply remain silent. But sometimes creating a plan for the future may mean acknowledging that the future will be worse before it gets better. Clearly acknowledge those risks and challenges up front. Doing so may allow you to avoid some risk factors and bolster your credibility. In contrast, missing your numbers or overrunning your budget erodes everyone's confidence in the project. By giving conservative time and profitability estimates, you can increase the chances that you will not go over deadlines or miss financial projections. Plus, change results that are better than expected can be celebrated as an even greater success. That's good planning for uncertainty, in a nutshell: Acknowledge the risks and challenges. Lay out your plan. Don't underestimate the time and resources required, and then rally your troops to deliver.

All of this requires being thorough in your projections and helping people see the big picture. To balance the fact that any bold change initiative will be full of uncertainty, it must offer significant benefits to the organization. It must provide a compelling return on the capital that is being invested. In other words, don't take on a bold, risky project with a $10 million investment for an estimated return of $12 million or even $15 million. For that level of investment, you probably want to go into it expecting a

$25–$30 million payback. Then, if you meet unexpected over-runs in time and money, there is still a reasonable likelihood that your now $14 million project is still a worthwhile investment. This is why venture capitalists typically won't even look at projects with less than a 30 percent internal rate of return and a better-than-four-times multiple on invested capital. They know that most surprises don't improve the economics of returns; instead, they depress them. Adopt a similar philosophy and don't even begin down the path of disruptive change unless the potential ultimate success has a payback sufficient to justify the time, energy, resources, and risk.

Finally, remember that any bold change is likely to require other resources in addition to capital. Even if these resources exist within the organization (for example, vacant facilities, spare work space, technical support, accounting), they must also be described and included in the budget.

People

Beyond physical resources, of course, you need the right people. This goes back to finding your pioneers and getting them on board quickly, since you need people who are committed, excited, and willing to put in the extra time and effort. In some stretches, you may need to get twelve-hour days for the price of eight, seven-day weeks for the price of five. The unfortunate fact is that success in transformative change initiatives in established companies doesn't usually produce extraordinary economic windfalls for the employees involved. It can, however, produce great amounts of psychic income that will keep the team engaged and productive. For this, you need people who appreciate the project for its intrinsic value—the purpose, the *why* behind the change—rather than solely for monetary compensation.

The mission and people's connection to it can be enormous assets, whatever the financial budget of the company or of its people. If the impetus that the mission provides is compelling and people see that their work matters, not just to the company's bottom line but to their community or the world at large, their rewards are not just financial. The depth of the mission is important, for as Terry Pearce has frequently reminded me, "People will give effort for money, but they will give their lives for meaning."

Preparing for Risks and the Inevitable Questions

Disruptive change takes time—and it takes even longer if things go wrong. The advance thinking and planning of Step Four can help you navigate through a number of barriers, but not all. The planning process you undertake in Step Five is perhaps the best time to take a preventive look at risk factors, to analyze and attempt to mitigate them proactively. Assessing and planning for risks is not a once-and-done task. It is a constant activity since conditions change and new risks can arise anytime from a host of places, both outside and inside the company. Outside obstacles such as regulatory changes or strategic moves by competitors can drop roadblocks in your path that are generally harder to anticipate than the internal risks leaders face in bringing an initiative to the world.

The sheer number of outside complications that might influence your organization make it virtually impossible to develop enough Plan Bs to counter every vulnerability from the outside. You must constantly plan ahead and be vigilant in looking for early indications that adversity lurks on the horizon. You should also expect your colleagues to ask you, "What might go wrong, and what will you do about it?" Be prepared to answer these questions. You can have contingency plans ready for the most likely problems. You also have to demonstrate that you've thought about even the risks you can't control and developed logical reactions.

Fortunately, anticipating and managing through internal risk factors is typically more straightforward than dealing with the external kind. Over the course of my career, I have sorted the internal risk factors of bold change into seven planning categories:

- Scope creep
- Technological stretch
- Corporate familiarity with the project
- Maintaining the team through the project
- Keeping management on board
- Investment size
- The quality of the planning effort

Developing an awareness of and a plan for these problems won't save you if something in the market goes awry or a competitor scoops you, but it will allow you to protect your project structure from internal hindrances that you can manage or even avoid.

Scope creep is ever present. Its risks exist right to the conclusion of the initiative. To those not responsible for leading the change, adding new elements to a significant change initiative can seem productive and logical. Since we are already changing so much, why not add a few more things to the list? Furthermore, as your success starts to take hold, new ideas to build on this success will blossom. Some of these additions can seem very beneficial, but you will have to stand firm on the boundaries of the change and resist additions that could overwhelm the focus of the project. This is not easy; it is even harder if some of the pressure comes from your own team or even from the face in the mirror. Resist! Put these new ideas into Phase Two or Release 2.0 of your initiative.

The technological stretch and its risks must be contextualized more than one way. Essentially, you want to take this query through three descending levels:

- Has this technological change ever been done anywhere?
- Has it ever been done in your industry?
- Has it ever been done in your organization?

As you can imagine, the risk decreases steadily as you get closer and closer to your organization. The more commonly used a technology is, the easier it will be to find the talent and experience required to be successful. If this is something that has been done in the industry, you might already have reliable consultants to bring on your team. Even better, if something similar has already been done in your organization, you may be able to readily access expertise within your own organization via a reassignment or loan. But if the change you are proposing involves something that has never or rarely been done before anywhere, you are taking on a much larger risk. Evaluating whether the "bleeding edge" is worth the potential risk is a very tough call.

Corporate familiarity with the project's business focus is the flip side of familiarity with the technological stretch and the questions are quite similar:

- Has a project like this ever been done anywhere?
- Has it ever been done in your industry?
- Has it ever been done in your organization?

You need to know if the company has done anything similar from a business model or conceptual design perspective. Is what you are proposing totally foreign to the people within your organization? What about the managerial structure? The cultural implications?

In suggesting that we change how the Schwab branch offices interacted with customers, I failed to realize how novel the change might appear. What I proposed was absolutely nothing new within the traditional brokerage industry, but it required behavior that was essentially the opposite of what our employees had always done. They had to become proactive rather than simply be reactive. A change that is foreign to the company can work, but since it's going to take longer and cost far more as a result, it needs to generate sufficient benefits to be worth the effort.

Maintaining the team for your project as a group and as individual contributors demands a strategy since disruptive change initiatives are very challenging, especially for the members of the core team. The excitement and momentum that you have carefully built can evaporate as an initiative stretches into months and years. Difficulty, coupled with a protracted time frame, can put a lot of stress on team members, and can reduce their morale over time. Success, on the other hand, can be something of a double-edged sword. The more high-profile your project, and the more outstanding the results, the greater the likelihood that team members will be recruited for other opportunities both inside and outside the company.

Don't underestimate the degree to which long-duration projects can test your resolve and the resolve of everyone around you. The time and effort required to keep the morale of the team high are substantial—and absolutely necessary. Breakthrough change is a protracted process. By breaking the effort down into smaller components early on, as described in Step Six, you can reduce the impression of the project taking too long and maintain momentum.

Keeping management on board is critical. Just as you need to build and maintain excitement about the project among your team members, you need to do so at every level of the organization. Your competitors are certainly not sitting around and waiting to see what is next on the horizon; they are searching for it. Your superiors know that—and will likely not be comfortable with a change that plays out over an extended period of time with few, if any, interim results. The best way to prevent a loss of interest is to keep management in the loop at all times. Similarly, your shareholders, investors, suppliers, customers, bosses, and subordinates need information. You have to get them on board, build excitement about the project and its progress, and keep them looking forward. As you do this, the stakes go up. The higher the visibility, the more important success becomes to the organization—and to you.

The investment size of this bold change is key—and must be considered within the context of your organization. Is this a $2 million change or a $20 million change? Risk increases proportionately with size. And of course, financial size is a relative matter. To some organizations, a $5 million project is a rounding error; to others, it is a bet-the-company investment. You must determine what kind of impact a failure would have on the organization as a whole. Is this a bet-the-company change? Or is it, potentially, a storm that the company could weather? This is not to suggest that you shouldn't initiate bet-the-company changes—I've done it myself—but you may have to reconcile yourself to significant personal risk, as well as the risk to the organization as a whole. It is my personal belief that you don't financially bet the company unless competitive circumstances demand such a move and everyone in leadership is totally behind you.

The quality of the planning effort is foremost. If you have followed all the steps up to this point, you will have already mitigated this potential problem. Remember that too much optimism can have a detrimental effect on your ability to plan. But you can also sabotage your plans if you are unable to recognize potential problems and create contingency plans. Lastly, as will be discussed in Step Six, clear and consistent metrics that let you see the limitations and warning signs are critical. If you skimp on the legwork at the beginning, you may be blindsided by one or more of these risk factors later on.

As much as we try to identify and plan to deal with risk, there will always be uncertainty when we are breaking new ground— and we must learn to live with that uncertainty. Indeed, our ability to lead and inspire when the outcome is not at all guaranteed is an important part of this process. Thinking about risks in advance, having contingency plans in place, and learning to expect the unexpected will be enormously helpful when you have to act fast, whether because of changes in the business, the market, or other circumstances.

~~~~~

In leading change, advance planning is key, whatever the goal and whatever the future. We need to conduct assessments and create plans that will help get us from where we are to where we want to be and we need to be flexible enough to adapt along the way. We need to build in time to revisit our plans. Are they on track and operating well? If not, reassess, adjust, and stay alert for changes ahead. Also, be sure to plan for a category of "unknown unknowns," just as the engineers at NASA have for decades.

Even the most detailed of plans will inevitably need modification along the way. And often, as we'll see in Step Six, a plan improves by being partitioned into smaller, more readily managed pieces in order to increase the likelihood of early success, test the process, and build commitment and momentum for more extensive changes.

Partitioning the Project and Building Momentum via Metrics, Analytics, and Celebrations

FAR-REACHING CHANGE INITIATIVES CAN be hard to visualize, particularly if the gap between here and there, between the present and the future seems extraordinarily large. If a change seems abstract and out of focus, if your people can't visualize the future in real terms, how will they muster the urgency to undertake the journey? You have to be committed to your ultimate goal and able to make that goal crystal clear.

While it may seem relatively easy to get everyone all fired up in the beginning, the greater challenge is keeping spirits high as the project stretches on. You need ways to make the immediate steps clear and to help people—particularly those who may not have been involved in developing the vision but who will be crucial to its realization—see the path to the future in real, concrete terms. Enable people to see the end result with such clarity that they can act on their own. The less threatening, more compelling, and more achievable you make the process of accomplishing the change initiative, the more likely you are to meet with success. Consider and specifically define "success" and focus on measurable outcomes.

The strength and detail of the long-range planning you undertook in Step Five will help you get people on board and mobilized.

Here we look at ways to partition the initiative to build in successes, create and maintain momentum, support the bottom line, and keep everyone engaged over the long haul.

Planning for Interim Successes

One of the best ways to preserve the enthusiasm that you have generated early on is to divide a major change initiative into smaller phases, with shorter and intermediate-term goals and specific, clearly defined benefits. This "one step at a time" approach feels more manageable and thus easier for individuals to commit to. Ideally, each of these smaller goals will take less than twelve months, preferably closer to six months. They provide a series of checkpoints where you can celebrate interim successes on the road to a completed change. Initiatives without major deliverables in intervals of less than twelve months are much riskier to attempt, in part because it's extremely difficult—financially and emotionally—to wait beyond twelve months for a hint of success. Without at least a few interim successes, you run the risk of dissipating your team's momentum and energy. Employees, team members, or those you report to may simply lose faith in the project. If you aren't producing results—positive results—top management may begin to allocate fewer resources to the project.

Instead, by partitioning your project and planning for interim successes, you'll reap multiple benefits, not the least of which is that the planning required to break things up into a phased approach makes every other part easier—and makes for fewer surprises. Taking the time to plan in detail, dividing a large-scale plan into increments, enables you to anticipate and time each phase and measure the core deliverables that indicate success. A phased approach improves the quality of planning and, in the long term, can also make you a better, more detailed planner. More immediately, it enables you to show results and increase support for the initiative.

Know Your Key Results

When you're leading transformative change, the work of selling your vision of the future is never really done. You and your team must constantly pitch your change initiative, justify its existence, and provide evidence that you're on the right path. Visible, measurable evidence of success can help you overcome the nay-sayers. Progress reports and completed tasks are helpful—and actual interim deliverables that bring interim benefits to the company are most successful in building and maintaining project momentum.

What are your key results? If *you* don't know them, who does? You need to develop a culture in which everyone at every level is focused on the vision and the key results the organization has established as its goal. This enables your people to self-select appropriate actions that deliver the desired result and to think and act in ways to achieve the key results. With this, the path to success is easier and faster.

You may need to focus on the top three or four most important results to create the unity and team mind-set that are essential for accomplishing the bigger-picture objectives. Most leaders think they are clear about the desired results and feel they talk about results so much that people must have memorized them. Unfortunately, too often, even executive teams cannot uniformly articulate their top three key results and exactly how they're measuring them. In these cases, just imagine how misaligned the rest of their organizations may be.

The problems of disconnect and misalignment can be readily resolved by focusing on key results that are *meaningful, measurable,* and *memorable*. Meaningful so that everyone can link to them. Measurable to quantify the goal line. Memorable to keep them front of mind and enable people to take ownership for results.

Simply reiterating your key results will not get you there. Until you share detailed information with your team, neither you nor the team members can have a true sense of the level of progress you are making and the implication that has for what lies ahead.

What Are You Measuring?

There's a strong desire in business to measure everything with one simple question: how much money are we making right now? This is perilous thinking, however, because financial performance in the early steps of a project is rarely the best way, and certainly not the only way, to measure success. With a disruptive change, it's particularly important to measure the interim steps and goals along the way since the end goal of enhanced profitability could be a long time in coming. Fortunately, there are always other, more immediate factors we can track that will lead to profit improvement down the road.

The tug-of-war between senior leaders (or boards) who always want aggressive goals and "more for less" versus change leaders who try to determine what they realistically need and then add a cushion or a margin for error is ongoing. The all-encompassing changes that are often necessary demand something other than a strictly bottom-line financial approach. Why not instead focus on and debate the larger-picture future we are shooting for, how we would measure and define that success, and what that success would be worth to our organization? Having those discussions early will help us more clearly frame what it will take to get us there and whether that level of resource commitment and risk burden is merited. This kind of heartfelt discussion is healthy—and not practiced often enough.

Measuring Progress and Success: Using Big Data, Metrics, and Analytics

The goals for change—particularly for bold, breakthrough change—can often seem subjective and nebulous, especially to managers and operators. The leaders and high-level executives who are responsible for funding a given project want concrete, measurable indicators (historically referred to as "metrics") that tell them how a change is going.

Early in my career, those of us in direct-response marketing measured and analyzed everything we could. In that world, success was the difference between a response rate of 1.5 percent versus 2.5 percent. We were constantly trying to test and measure how much of that came from which part of marketing and promotion—new advertising, new slogans, new positioning, new product features, new media. The rise of big data has changed all that. The possibilities big data offers seem phenomenal; the opportunities to analyze enormous amounts of data in real time, very enticing. But what are the practicalities? How should leaders factor big data's potential into disruptive changes they're rolling out today? Big data can be gamed and distorted, and errors can easily be magnified even as the terms used may seem exact. And yet, big data is here and part of the business world.

Perhaps you have ready access to elements of big data that can be useful and easily tapped. If not, understand that building big data capabilities is a major change project in and of itself, and your project is undoubtedly challenging enough. Whether your company is new or old, you must be disciplined and pragmatic in what data you do go after, so that the data is manageable. TPG Capital's Steve Ellis emphasized the importance of understanding "the three to five most important metrics, the leading indicators, that have the highest correlation to the outcome you're after." Once you know that, invest the time to create real-time monitoring of "metrics that matter" so that you are aiming at the right target.

How do we best make use of the data and monitor the indicators? There are two major types of indicators—leading and lagging—each with different implications for your change initiative. Often indicators are analyzed simply by comparing current numbers to prior numbers. While period comparison and trending analysis can offer useful information, that information can be overly simplistic. For deeper, more thorough analysis, vintage and ratio analysis can provide valuable information. These concepts warrant further discussion.

Leading Indicators

As the name implies, leading indicators are harbingers or evidence of success or failure that appear before any of the others. A common misconception is that market share and profitability are leading indicators. In fact, it's more likely that we are hoping these will dramatically accelerate toward the end of the project; they rarely do so at the beginning.

If we've started rolling out a new web-based service, leading indicators might be represented by how many hits the website has received, how many people have logged in to the service, or how this data is trending over time. This information gives a sense of whether or not we're attracting new or existing customers with our website and whether we are getting the customer engagement that we want.

On a completely different track, we could also look at staff turnover. Did anyone quit last week? Last month? Last quarter? If so, how many and what did they describe as their reasons? This information can tell us how employees are adjusting to the change. These variations occur as a direct and immediate result of the changes we are implementing. We can measure these along with a host of other factors and follow their trends over time.

We must also pinpoint the leading indicators to clearly and proactively articulate the targets for each one to management and to employees. With those clarified, it will not appear that we are trying to justify any lagging profitability results down the road. Choose your indicators carefully, based on the nature of the project and with the understanding that too much data may overwhelm people and dilute the focus of your group's efforts. Potential leading indicators to track range from measures of customer and employee engagement to sales numbers and positive reviews.

Depending on the situation, some indicators can potentially be lagging indicators as well. For example, customer attrition may be a leading indicator in the sense that it's a problem you want to see beginning to decline as your new initiative takes hold. It can also be a lagging indicator since a new service or pricing approach may appeal to higher-potential customers but cause other customers to leave.

You will be measuring leading *and* lagging indicators, simultaneously, from the start of the project. Initially, the lagging indicators create the baseline to measure against as new trends eventually emerge. Your expectation is that the leading indicators will move first in the positive direction you are hoping for. Your project plan and economic forecast will require you to make a guess as to when the lagging indicators will begin to improve. Until they do, people may be on pins and needles, nervous about results; you must be the voice of confidence and reassurance to keep morale high. The time lapse between positive trends in leading indicators and clearly improved results in lagging indicators can be months and quarters if not even years. If leading indicators are disappointingly low, that same problem will likely be reflected in the final outcomes. Effectively measuring, tracking, and responding to the leading indicators is therefore critical.

Lagging Indicators

Lagging indicators are the big and important measures of success—such as reduced costs or improved market share, competitive position, pricing power, profit dollars, and profit margins—that we are working toward. Everyone wants to see positive lagging indicators and, typically, the sooner the better.

But the results reflected in lagging indicators take time, sometimes years, to emerge. They are almost always foreshadowed by positive trends with leading indicators.

There is huge pressure to see movement in the lagging indicators, no matter what the leading indicators are doing. This pressure comes from everywhere: Wall Street analysts, stockholders, boards, senior management, you name it. And the wait for results can seem interminable. So how do we help our people through that long period before the lagging indicators move? Analytics and measurements can help: the more precise and granular they are, the better. We want monthly, weekly, and even daily measurements. We want to see every emerging trend, and every reporting period counts. All this information can be used to help us make progress.

Vintage and Ratio Analysis

In comparison to leading and lagging indicators, *vintage analysis* is used less frequently. It is very powerful and immensely enlightening, and I believe it should be used more. With vintage analysis, one compares the performance of groups, or cohorts, of customers or employees to the performance of other groups over equivalent lengths of times in their gestation with the company. It is therefore a more sophisticated measure than simple year-over-year analysis. For example, you could compare the initial quarterly performance of all the sales executives who were hired and trained in the first quarter of *this* year with the initial quarterly results of those hired and trained in the first quarter of the *previous* year, thus comparing results from executives in the same stage of their maturity in the business. Is this year's cohort doing better or worse than last year's? If you have a major project and you need to train and reward the sales staff in new and different ways, track and review their performance by vintage. This tells you whether or not what you are doing differently is working, adding value, and worth the effort and cost.

We can also look at customers in this same way. If we consider every quarter's batch of new customers as a distinct cohort, or vintage, we can compare the characteristics of customers having equivalent levels of time with the company. Since customer life cycles are critical to most companies' success, this kind of analytic is essential because it allows you to determine if the performance of the newer vintage is better or worse.

Ratio analysis is an underutilized approach for measuring trends in business. In innovative change initiatives, we are hoping for significant trending improvements in outcomes versus inputs. But since the numbers are moving around so much, how should we analyze over various time frames? Ratios are an excellent way to do this. Obvious examples are sales per employee, revenues per customer or by customer segment, cost per lead, and close per lead. Also, you should be collecting data on measures of business (revenues, products purchased, new customers, and so forth) compared to website traffic and dollars spent to generate traffic. Essentially, you want to explore the relationship between inputs and outcomes over time and look for improving trends.

Sharing Goals, Results, and Progress

Just as we want the goals to be clearly defined, we want the results to be highly visible so that everyone can see the progress in real time. Progress posters and plaques on the wall are old school—and still very effective. We can also keep updates current on a video screen that employees see daily and use the digital possibilities: e-mail updates, phone updates, social media, tweeting. Making the analytics visible to the point of near inescapability is always useful. It's more challenging if the direction is negative or ambiguous rather than positive, but still necessary.

Setting out information for leading indicators and your most significant lagging indicator helps make the need for change real and can turn skeptics into believers who pitch in and gear up for the challenge. Once everyone can measure their work product against a competitive set of outcomes, results will rise, along with excitement and enthusiasm within the team.

The more visually powerful the display of information, the less team members can deny it. In addition to indicating how the team at large is doing, you can show how individual staff members are performing. Take the company culture into account and experiment with different approaches, such as comparing regional teams or displaying only the standings of individuals who are above the mean score of the group. But facts are what they are, and we all have to be held accountable for our results.

Having successfully used visible rankings with a region that had been ranked last, I know it works. As is often the case, the region's ranking was low not because the team was full of terrible people, but because it was full of people who had not challenged old ways of doing things, looked for new processes and ideas, or strived to meet a higher standard. The potential was there; we just needed a spark to get going. The posters helped, but the real spark came when the leadership team stood before the employee group (of about 100 people) and expressed our willingness to be held accountable for significantly improving our results, and our conviction that we could succeed together. Even the most tenured of the managers committed to do things in new ways and to drive our rankings higher. We had to develop and implement real ideas for how to do things better—and we did. We instituted some major changes and piloted new ideas. At first these innovations faced significant resistance internally. But as people began to see the logic and as the momentum from our success grew, so did the willingness of the team to do things differently.

Making a change happen is a massive undertaking, deeply rooted in social and emotional issues. We are managing emotions. We are managing passion. We are managing people's energy and commitment to the change. It's very powerful to be able to take all that critical data and hang it up on the wall or display it on a video screen for everyone to see. Every day, an employee can come in and think, "I'm proud of my personal position," or "I need to work harder here." Throughout, the leaders must take every opportunity to encourage and guide people to improve.

It's logical to fixate on the people who are most immediately vital to your project: your team members and your management. But without customers, your change initiative may never make it to completion, no matter how groundbreaking and positive it is in theory. If you've recently lost customers, quickly determine why and focus attention on their needs, perhaps by first attending to a part of the overall change initiative that will bring them back. In fact, large changes often come out of some sort of deficiency in the way that your organization is serving the customer. While you're working to correct that deficiency, customers are still experiencing the old way of doing business; you may need to create an improved method of serving them in the interim. You could pull someone from the team to problem-solve, but bringing in an outside expert may get you to the answer quickly and smoothly, and without taking a team member's time and focus. Even a quick fix can have a huge impact on the economics and the project momentum. Finding interim successes while creating value for the customers at the same time is a plus for the customers and for the company's bottom line.

Building in Celebrations

In addition to the numbers, be sure to celebrate and recognize the individual stories of personal sacrifice and commitment to the mission. These are the stories that people remember, and in telling these stories to the team, leaders have the opportunity to share their thinking with respect to movement in results and growing success. More importantly, by paying attention to and celebrating stories of personal sacrifice and commitment, we can genuinely demonstrate our gratitude to team members who are pouring their hearts and souls into our collective success, while we recognize and thank them for being role models for all of us.

Don't let a success, even a small interim success, slide under the radar unnoticed. From both a career and psychological perspective, people need to be seen to have accomplishments. Without a sense of accomplishment and achievement within the team, burnout can easily become a problem. Acknowledging and celebrating small, staggered successes boosts morale and helps with team retention. Further, each celebration can reinforce the overall goal. Particularly if that goal is far on the horizon, actively look for and create small celebrations in each phase of the initiative to help keep the team energized and spur forward momentum.

Everyone must be on board and focused on the right goals and values for the innovative change to succeed. Getting people to believe and having them be all in is critical, for culture drives everything. Improvements do not happen by accident or by luck, but from a detailed plan and active involvement. In celebrating the interim successes, you can build momentum for the move to the future. Interim successes can—and do—make all the difference.

~~~~~

Disruptive change is often about a new way of doing business, a new distribution channel, a new product, a new position in the market. As you develop your plan, carefully consider which interim steps you will focus on first. How will you capture what you've learned from those steps and celebrate the interim successes? How will you increase and maintain momentum? How will you fund it all?

The steps enable you to anticipate potential delays and prepare yourself and your team for surprises, both of which could add expense and time to the project. Measurement, metrics, and analytics play a key role in supporting the overall plan and reinforcing support for the initiative, which must be done continuously. From leading and lagging indicators to big data to various types of analyses, the available information is nonstop. Determine what's most important among competing issues and direct your attention there. Often it will seem the only thing top management cares about is enhanced profitability—and in many ways, that's true. But a narrow, myopic fixation on profitability alone can test your resolve, lead you to make rash course corrections, and possibly have you heading off in the wrong direction. If the leading indicators are slow to move, look for evidence of improvement and make it visible in anecdotal stories. Shine a light on behaviors and attitudes that support the change. By encouraging this progress, you'll reinforce confidence and increase momentum. These stories are typically dramatically more compelling than statistics; further, they increase emotional energy and can help the group persevere.

Leading a disruptive change is fundamentally about creating and managing both the actual momentum and the perception of momentum. Ultimately, the lagging indicators of growing profitability, margins, market share, and market position must appear. But this can take years. In the meantime, agreeing on the leading indicators and measuring and celebrating them along the way will build and maintain momentum for the change initiative among the larger team. And if leading indicators or other situations improve your projections, be sure to quantify the benefit. You can then essentially reinvest in your own project, using the money you've saved or produced with these smaller, incremental changes to support a pilot and the entire rollout effort, discussed in Steps Seven and Eight.

Testing with Pilots to Increase Success

T HE PREMISE UNDERLYING *Driving Disruption* is that by carefully considering and executing each of the steps, you pave the way for success in implementing the change you are championing. The rest should be easy, right?

Not always. By its nature, disruptive change can be challenging every single step of the way. The pilot and the rollout stages (which naturally overlap) are no exception—and they are critically important.

Innovative change can manifest in many forms: a new product, a new process for doing things, a new business model, a new technology platform, geographic expansion into new markets, even changes we haven't yet imagined. Defining a precise set of rules about how to roll out your next change initiative is impossible: the potential projects are simply too diverse. Nevertheless, appropriate and careful use of pilot projects is a consistent thread in successful rollouts. The focus of Step Seven is therefore on how to successfully employ pilot implementations to enhance your prospects for success.

A caveat: much as I strongly advocate using pilot projects, there are instances when it may seem you have no choice but to simply go forward with your change and forgo any testing. Sometimes you have to balance the urgency of the need against the possible benefits of a pilot. For example, with our internet trade pricing change at Schwab, there was just too much urgency and our pricing was too visible and transparent for us to test the pricing change with different market geographies or customer segments. More typically, however, there are plenty of opportunities to employ pilot implementations and no shortage of good reasons to do so.

Pilot Projects Are Key

Pilots have historically been a big part of change initiatives. They provide ways to run small, select tests to determine if the proposed change is feasible and viable. They help you test to see if you'll get the desired effects and business advantages. Pilots can be run in different manners, different locations, different phases of the project, and for different purposes. Certain pilots are very specific to types of businesses.

The focus here is on pilots that test significant changes to many aspects of a company's business model or production processes (versus technology pilots or software beta tests). If a company's training programs were shown to need major revisions and updating, a company might run pilot trainings for one module in different formats. This would enable the company to get a head start on training and determine which of the formats—one-on-one training, in-class instruction, online instruction, or some combination—is the most efficient and cost-effective in transmitting the desired information and skills. The following sections describe traditional proof of concept pilots, scalability pilots, and one that is particular to both *Stacking the Deck* and *Driving Disruption*.

Traditional Proof of Concept Pilots

Traditional proof of concept pilots rest on a belief that it makes the most sense to test a new idea on a representative sample of your customers and your employees. If you're a nationwide company in the United States, you want to launch a pilot in locations on both coasts, in the Southeast, Southwest, Midwest, and Rockies. You want to use some of your best managers, some middle-of-the-road managers, some high-performing locations, and some average ones. The goal is to create a slice of life and then see how your idea performs in this micro but representative version of the real world.

How you structure this pilot and interpret the results can make or break a project over the long run. If an ordinary proof of concept pilot—directed toward a typical cross section of your customer base and run by a typical cross section of your employees—fails, if your customers don't take to it or your management has trouble implementing it, it's natural to rationalize that failure. By the time you get to implementing the pilot step, you've already invested enormously in your change initiative. You believe deeply in the urgent need for this change and have spent time and energy on it. You have devoted yourself to inspiring others to believe in the urgency and viability of this change. You have put yourself on the line with your superiors or the board advocating for this change. Even if the data suggests weakness, it can be hard to scrutinize, let alone walk away from, the effort. You are primed to ignore or dismiss evidence that the initiative is flawed. This is a very natural reaction, just not at all helpful.

After a failed pilot, it's easy to focus on the fact that there are many variables, many reasons an un-optimized pilot could fail outside of a fundamental flaw with the concept. When an ordinary proof of concept pilot fails, you wind up with a lot of potential questions, such as:

- Was the incentive package we offered not sufficiently attractive?
- Was the training flawed? In what way?
- What did we overlook that we should have included?
- Did we not give the team enough money to implement the pilot successfully?
- Was the timeline too short?

But none of these questions and others that might come up after the fact really get at the meat of whether or not your change is fundamentally a good idea, one that can work. Even when the right action might be a very basic reconsideration of the change effort, the tendency is to modify some of the variables and go back to the market with another, similarly structured traditional proof of concept pilot.

In addition, even the best proof of concept pilot is typically far removed from a test of scalability, the ability to take the change to the full breadth of the company's business. Since many big change efforts fail due to an inability to successfully scale the change, it's important not to shortchange the piloting phase or bring the change to the marketplace too quickly. Traditional proof of concept pilots and scalability pilots are both critical. But in my opinion, these shouldn't be the first pilots undertaken as your initial test in the real world.

From Proof of Concept
to Stacked Proof of Concept Pilots

I recommend adding an even earlier, smaller pilot, designed in every way to succeed. I call this a *stacked proof of concept pilot* because it is optimally configured to give your change, your idea, every possible opportunity to succeed. Instead of a wide range of geographical locations, you select the best possible location, where people (potential customers and staff alike) will be most receptive to the proposed change. You target your ideal customer base, those segments most likely to respond positively. And you handpick your best and brightest managers and employees, gathering people who are drawn to and thrive on change, who are actively excited about innovation. Everyone you choose to be involved in the pilot team should be enthusiastic, forward thinking, and completely on board with the change.

If you have thoroughly set up your stacked proof of concept pilot and it fails, you are forced to concede that since your idea can't succeed here, it probably can't succeed *anywhere* and needs to be fundamentally reconsidered. On the other hand—while your results cannot yet be projected across the organization—a success gives you great advantages in attacking *the next stage* of the pilot process.

Starting with a stacked proof of concept pilot before undertaking a more typical proof of concept pilot allows you to guard against rationalizations. By removing all possible implementation issues, individual motivation issues, and employee pushback issues, the stacked proof of concept pilot lets you test the single question: can this idea work? Better to fail fast, shake it off, learn, and go forward.

One criticism of an optimized, or stacked, proof of concept pilot is that by its very nature (using only the best and the brightest and backing them with all the available resources), it doesn't provide information about how the idea performs in average or poor situations. True: it's not a mirror of reality. But why not be better prepared before you take on reality? Why not gather as much information as you can before tackling a major change, so that you and your team can significantly increase your chances to succeed? A stacked proof of concept pilot enables you to do just that. It's not a license to roll out the implementation company-wide. Instead it's a confirmation that your idea is viable, and it's a bit of preemptive insurance against big, public failure that could be incredibly difficult for the team or the company to bounce back from.

If you are lucky enough to have the resources, you could test more than one stacked proof of concept pilot. The choices you make in stacking the pilot are your best guesses—and determining an optimal configuration is relatively easy. Management typically knows where its best people, strongest business conditions, and situations most receptive to innovation are. If you can conduct more than one stacked proof of concept pilot, either simultaneously or serially, perhaps in different locations or focusing on different demographics, so much the better.

Naturally, the process doesn't end with a stacked proof of concept pilot or even a subsequent more traditional proof of concept pilot. Eventually, you will want to conduct a scalability pilot for viability on a large scale. Before turning to scalability pilots, we'll explore a few other points about testing.

Testing Assumptions, Minimizing Risks,
and Gaining Advocates

Any sort of test is about validating or refuting assumptions. Therefore, before starting a pilot implementation of any sort, we should have a good sense of what assumptions we have, and thus the questions to ask. As just a few examples:

- We are assuming this change will make us more productive. Will it? By how much?
- We're assuming that customers will respond positively to this initiative. Will they?
- We are assuming that we can win over the employees. Can we?

A stacked proof of concept pilot can answer these questions and potentially force us to reevaluate our plan for implementing the change. For example, let's say we start our best managers in our best locations for the pilot. These highly skilled individuals know how to motivate and inspire their people, who in turn trust their leadership. If these top managers can't get their people on board, then our average manager is really going to struggle—and may not get anywhere with the project. We might reevaluate the amount of time we budget to get our employees behind the change. Maybe instead of two weeks of training and support we should plan for a month or even two or more. Or reconsider the entire implementation plan.

Rather than diving in with a big change, better to test your proposed changes, learn along the way, and build momentum. Time spent in pilots testing assumptions and gathering facts is time well spent since it enables you to avoid risks and damages you might not have anticipated.

Beyond testing assumptions, what else can a pilot offer? You want to know everything possible about how the implementation is working—or not—for your employees and your customers. It is often useful, after a pilot, to bring your managers together and ask them how they felt about the process:

- Did they feel that the training was adequate?
- What, if anything, did they learn from the process?
- Did they get frustrated? When? Why?
- Did the system, process, product, or idea actually work?
- How did the customers react?
- How did the employees react?
- What could the leadership team do better?

These questions and more are important to bring out in the open. Surprises are deadly when you are implementing transformative change; every question you answer early is one less surprise down the road. Another plus is that the people who lead the pilot effort and come from the field can now advocate with their peers for this new idea. Once actual frontline employees are actively supporting the new idea, progress toward company-wide acceptance of the change can speed up.

By using multiple pilots either in sequence or in staggered stages, conducting separate pilots for different phases of the overall plan, you can speed up the entire rollout dramatically and begin seeing improvement in indicators early on. Another benefit of using multiple or staggered pilots is that just as you never get all the time and resources you want, you may rarely get enough money to roll out a big change all at once. If the overall change is going to happen in a series of steps anyway, it makes sense to learn everything you can from each individual step.

From Proof of Concept to Scalability Pilots and Beyond

Of course, just as in any other strategy, wishful thinking can lead to an unsupportable reliance on pilots. Putting too much emphasis on a proof of concept pilot can lead people to move directly into execution mode too soon. You must do more than simply prove whether the idea works or not. You must be able to create a scaled commercial implementation of that model. Referred to as a scaled pilot or a scalability pilot, this step of testing the model on a broader scale is critical.

You must exploit every opportunity to increase the probability of success. One success does not guarantee another and even the greatest proof of concept pilot should not be relied on as definitive proof that a larger rollout will be destined to succeed. Don't declare victory on the strength of one pilot. That pilot may tell you the idea *can* work; you still need to test whether the concept is truly scalable, whether it *will* work.

Pilots Demand Constant Evaluation and Coordination

This emphasis on the types of pilot tests that are equally critical and must be conducted is intentional. Unless you appreciate the differences, you run the risk of doing one without the other. Or overvaluing one over the other. Or simply not running enough pilots for thorough testing.

No matter how convincing your stacked proof of concept pilot, once it's complete, be sure to consider the roles of traditional proof of concept pilots and scalability pilots. Often, however, there isn't time to implement these in three separate phases. If that's the case, combining a traditional proof of concept and a scalability pilot is certainly possible—as long as you pay careful attention to what you measure and how you measure and plan. You must think about a representative sampling of your average locations or management teams or customer segments well before rolling the project out full scale. Be sure to take the time to test your idea in the crucible of unresponsive customers, resistant employees, and less receptive locations. A stacked proof of concept pilot requires you to nurture your idea and give it every shot at success; a scalability pilot requires you to test and prepare for the implementation challenges that lie ahead. Once you know the idea can work, you must learn how to make it work in situations that are less than ideal, if not outright challenging.

Understand the different types of pilots and their usefulness in a variety of situations and you can save everyone time and effort. One of the greatest benefits of pilots—and the multiple pilot systems—is that they enable us to discover problems and develop solutions while the scale is still limited and more manageable. This is important since there are always some things we can't fully understand until we do them, problems that can't be foreseen, new challenges we didn't expect.

Looking to the Future

As we look ahead to where a huge amount of innovation will come from, we see a tidal wave of the human–technology interaction, which we are still trying to imagine, plan for, build, and exploit. In researching for the future—starting, even leaping toward it— we explore the ideas and test to see where the greatest benefits may be, all while anticipating that once we have developed a clear strategy, the technology will not be far behind. While the progress today in hardware is impressive, the progress in software-based services and solutions is especially noteworthy. The world of apps, the world of mobility and connectivity, is moving at light speed and is likely to accelerate as we transform business processes and whole industries.

How does this world intersect with pilot implementations? If you're working in research and development at a high-tech company, you will sometimes create the front end of a project so that the consumer interaction looks smooth, polished, and fast enough to be computer-run, when in fact the back end is being handled manually. Effectively, this is a pilot of a pilot, enabling you to test the worth of an idea, the kernel of an innovation, and the various avenues of the process very early. It helps you see and explore the consumers' reactions, what they like and what they don't like. It lets you discover whether the idea resonates in the market before you expend the time and money perfecting the software, and long before you attempt to take the project to scale. Running a project in this way enables you to get ahead of where the world is (in this particular respect) and explore possibilities. It allows you to test the validity of an idea and learn, via experience, what details and processes will ultimately need to be built into the technology.

~~~~~

Pilots can be used in a variety of ways and combinations. They let you perfect the nuts and bolts of the process for your change initiative and dramatically increase the likelihood of its overall success. If you've prepared carefully and a pilot falls flat—if there's a fundamental flaw in the project—take the opportunity to learn and pivot. The information you glean from a pilot is never wasted; instead, a failed pilot is a lesson, one that has averted the potential disaster of a failed project.

Use pilots early and often to unearth any problems with your change initiative and to develop necessary revisions. As you partition your project, you may find that phases and segments of the plan can be tested with pilots or multiple staggered pilots. Test your assumptions, test the market, test your concept thoroughly before you even consider taking it to full scale—and use a scalability pilot before going to full rollout.

After investing time and energy preparing to bring about an innovative change, some leaders make the mistake of looking at the pilot step as a kind of gateway and believe that a successful pilot indicates a clear passage to full implementation. This is flawed thinking. A pilot is a chance to acquire valuable information not typically available in any other way. It is a gift that helps you and your team be well prepared as you move toward the future you envision.

Once you and your team are confident that your change initiative is ready to be introduced or rolled out to the real world, carefully consider how you will do this. Even the most well-conceived and well-constructed changes demand meticulous attention through the rollout and beyond. We'll investigate this further in Step Eight.

Pulling the Steps Together

THINK HOW QUICK AND easy change would be if we could simply move from one step to the next, with each step getting us an exact portion of the way to the desired change. But the steps of the *Driving Disruption* process are neither literal nor linear. Instead you'll undertake some parts simultaneously. Occasionally you'll double back, to reconsider a previous step based upon the work in a subsequent step. In that sense, the steps are somewhat fluid in ways that can work to your advantage—now that you're alert to the process. Here we examine how the steps fit together and build on each other and we delve into additional topics that will further prepare you to successfully lead disruptive change.

The starting point for a transformative change initiative typically involves a very small circle of executives—and within that group, these steps can be considered as fairly linear. Looking ahead to determine what skills and experiences will be required once it's time to expand the circle of active participants and bring more voices, players, and perspectives into the process is key. If you will need to go outside the company to recruit, this could consume considerable amounts of time, money, and effort, so getting an early handle on your needs and working in parallel with the other steps is very important.

As we progress through the steps, we must revisit Step One and communicate the need for change to the broader team, along with the vision of the future that we developed in Step Three.

Our work on the barriers described in Step Four, particularly the section on planning for the unexpected, leads into the planning process of Step Five and the partitioning and metrics of Step Six, which build upon each other and connect to support transformative change. Over time, we will repeat and revise aspects of these steps, including the pilots of Step Seven. Essentially, the process remains incomplete until all the steps have been laid out and thoroughly enumerated.

The steps usually begin in the order as presented in this book. Figure 8.1 illustrates how the steps that precede rollout might be sequenced relative to each other. Precise timing depends on circumstances and resources. There will naturally be some amount of overlap among steps and parallel work efforts along the way. After all, if disruptive change were a straightforward, lockstep process, experienced leaders certainly wouldn't constantly emphasize how difficult it is.

Leading with Conviction

To inspire and drive transformative change, you must have a deep, enduring conviction about the importance of the change you're pursuing. Sometimes leadership is the only force that keeps the change moving, so you must believe in it, to your core. The change process is a long road, so long that leaders often underestimate what it takes. It's tough to accurately define what bold change really is and what it really demands. Much as we might hope for an easier path, getting human beings to change is really, really hard.

Making it through the ebbs in conviction, the dips in morale when people are struggling through the pain of the change without yet seeing the benefit, can be particularly perilous. If these dips continue, the will to change can dissipate even before people on the front lines have changed the way they do things. And the outcome you were looking for will not materialize. Whether you are in the boardroom or managing operations on the ground, as a leader you need the conviction, the determination, the emotional endurance, and the energy to see the change through.

Negotiating Terms

In driving disruptive change, the CEO must first negotiate with the board regarding expectations. But what of the operator who

Active leadership involvement

Ongoing activity with the broader team

1 Establishing the need to change and a sense of urgency

2 Assembling and unifying your leadership team

3 Developing and communicating a clear and compelling vision of the future

4 Planning ahead for known and unknown barriers

5 Creating and managing a workable plan

6 Partitioning the project and building momentum

7 Testing with pilots to increase success

Early thinking and preliminary action

8 Pulling the steps together

Figure 8.1 Sequencing and Coordinating the Steps

109

will be tasked with leading the change on the ground? Imagine a major initiative that might just transform the future of your organization. Your superiors have already navigated Steps One and Three. They are looking to complete Step Two by filling out the leadership team and get the project rolling. The project involves a certain level of risk, and to mitigate that vulnerability, they need a strong, capable leader to organize the initiative. You know all this only because your boss has just informed you that you have been selected to lead this critical and very risky initiative. What do you do?

You may well be eager to launch your project and get a sense of exactly what it requires, while shoring up your own bargaining position with some incremental successes. But starting too quickly may be a mistake. You have the most leverage *before* the project begins—perhaps before you even formally sign on. Before you irrevocably accept this assignment and get rolling, you should thoughtfully assess the resources you have been assigned and establish clear parameters of success and failure for your efforts. The board may have seen the big picture, but you need to carefully consider the steps as you begin the process of negotiation. Resources, deadlines, deliverables, and decision rights are the major terms to codify and agree upon early in the process.

It's tempting to think that success and failure are clear, distinct, and self-evident. A project that invests $5 million and makes $12 million is a success, right? But what if it was supposed to make $20 million? The difference between success and failure can be completely in the eye of the beholder. How we set and negotiate expectations with our superiors or with shareholders and analysts can determine whether a change is hailed as a huge success; seen as long overdue; or, much worse, too little too late.

You want to lead this project but as you hear about the thinking that's already begun to develop, your sense is that the expected outcomes are entirely too aggressive. They want too much, too fast, and with too few of the resources you believe are necessary. This is nothing new in business. Leadership is all about setting extremely high expectations and then inspiring the team to strive toward success. You can't simply communicate deadlines and deliverables upwards; instead, negotiate from a place of strength and knowledge to secure the best possible framework for your project.

Be aware that you may be setting yourself up for difficulty and disappointment if you agree to take the project as is. Disappoint sky-high expectations, and it will be seen as your fault, rather than the result of overly ambitious initial terms. The time to set the terms is at the outset of the initiative. You may not be able to get everything you want or need in the beginning. But a thorough conversation early on can help you discover where there is give. The deadline may be dictated by competitive realities or already negotiated and set at a higher level of the organization. But perhaps the deliverable can be scaled back to a pilot implementation or a limited-scale rollout that will require less time and money than a full implementation. Decision rights are more flexible and may be the most dependent on early negotiation. You need to know what decisions you are allowed to make, how fast you can move, and when exactly you need to get higher-level approvals. If you establish yourself as someone willing to accept an extraordinary amount of managerial oversight without argument or wait until your project is already under way to begin asserting yourself, you will find it very difficult to get away from that initial perception.

As the leader of this phase of the change initiative, you will be held responsible for its outcome. You must therefore negotiate carefully up front, nailing down as many issues as possible, with as much precision as possible. Just as you have to carve out your own authority, you must do so for your people. Be very clear with your team members about where their responsibilities and duties begin and end—and don't make the mistake of postponing these conversations.

When you take on leading this change, you take on responsibility for any development and may be held accountable for decisions you neither made nor recommended. Keep the big picture in mind and control what you can.

Getting Started

Whether you are the CEO or the operator driving the change, it's important to "go slow to go fast." Greater diligence in the early planning stages of a project may allow multiple teams to work simultaneously on multiple threads and achieve a significant effort for less money and in a shorter amount of elapsed time. For those of us who are eager to get going, who can't wait for the future, this can be a very difficult concept to embrace.

Until some particularly strong form of resistance pops up to remind me, my instinct is more typically to "go fast and then go faster." To overcome this shortcoming, I rely on diversity in the leadership team and have surrounded myself with people who fully understand the importance of going slowly and carefully at the outset and who know to push back when my instincts for speed get in the way. Whatever skills you are working on, be sure you've included people whose strengths counterbalance your weaknesses. Beyond filling in your own gaps, recognize that seeing diversity in the leadership team encourages those throughout the larger organization; seeing themselves reflected there can inspire people to put forth their best efforts.

Once the leadership team is on board at the beginning of big, innovative change initiatives, many (if not most) of these leaders will want to get rolling and begin to see change actually happening. But the slow, methodical steps of mapping out such an effort are exactly what is needed. Anything else will result in disappointment and wasted time, effort, and money.

In addition to the reminders to go slow to go fast, the principles described in Geoffrey Moore's classic, *Crossing the Chasm*, can be immensely helpful. Often, especially in the high-tech world, you can find an audience who will adopt almost any new idea. These "early adopters," as Moore refers to them, will overcome bugs, inconveniences, poor service, inadequate instructional manuals, and other difficulties to have the latest technology. They buy new product concepts early, not for the novelty or to be first, but because they can "imagine, understand, and appreciate the benefits."

The early adopters are not enough. You must also appeal to Moore's "early majority," the roughly one-third of potential customers who simply won't tolerate the glitches or problems that early adopters accept. Without this middle group, you can't attract the "late majority" (the final third) who watch and wait, not buying until the product or program "has become an established standard."

In many ways, the ideas Moore presents parallel the ideas behind proof of concept versus scalability pilots. Just because something works once or works with a select group does not mean it is ready for widespread rollout and the harsh test of mainstream reality. There are chasms between groups; it's crossing those chasms that presents the challenges. Whether our initial success comes from a pilot or a rollout to the early adopters, success comes from building momentum and recognizing that early initial success is just that. It's the beginning of bringing the initiative out to the world, not the end.

Balancing the Risk of Failure

When we talk about innovative, disruptive change and pioneers, we must inevitably talk about the risk of failure—perhaps even failure on a large scale. Even with all the advance planning and preparation you've done through the steps, transformative change carries risks. Your people are going to be nervous about the prospect of risking their careers and reputations on untested ideas. What then should a leader say when asked, "What are the personal consequences if we are not successful here? Is it okay to fail?"

These are difficult questions. Leaders certainly can't say, "Sure, it's perfectly okay to fail!" because usually it's not. Saying something like, "Well, it depends." is more of a non-answer and doesn't really offer any useful or reassuring guidance. Instead, consider the concept of Noble Failure.

As the Irish poet, critic, and educator Edward Dowden (1843–1913) put it, "Sometimes a noble failure serves the world as faithfully as a distinguished success." But who decides if a failure is "noble"?

In an attempt to better answer the often-unstated questions about failure, I have elaborated on the concept of Noble Failure and given it specific conditions, recognizing that bold change initiatives inevitably run the risk of failing. Often the failure is not a result of incompetence or lack of effort; instead, it is due to any number of factors over which you have limited control. Projects can still fail even if you carefully go through every step in the *Driving Disruption* process. Perhaps the idea behind your initiative was fundamentally flawed. Or as you were in the middle of the project, another company came out with a superior product. These are the kinds of risks that you can never fully avoid or neutralize. We need a new category of failure to describe such situations.

Noble Failure, in my view, has seven important conditions:

1. The project was *well planned.* You did your homework and you crunched the numbers. You used intuition only where appropriate.
2. You *failed smart and small.* Whenever possible, you confined your failure to the lab or a pilot program. You used

models and prototypes and conducted lower-cost tests whenever feasible.

3. You had a *contingency plan*. You knew the places where the plan was most likely to get off track and were prepared to slow it down and steer carefully through the curves if necessary.

4. You *didn't bet the company*. Your failure didn't cost so much money that the company is now in financial trouble. You considered opportunities to syndicate the risk with other organizations if appropriate.

5. You *limited the negative fallout*. This failure was not hugely public; it didn't cause a compliance, legal, or PR fiasco. You did not imperil the company's reputation.

6. You followed a policy of "*no surprises*" with your superiors. If the project was struggling, you let management know so they could potentially help you or prepare contingency plans you had not thought of.

7. *You learned from your experience*. You conducted a post-mortem and tried to extract learning opportunities from this experience both for yourself and for the organization.

If each of these principles has been considered and practiced in depth before, during, and after the effort, the change may be thought of as a Noble Failure. In that case, what we don't do is punish the person or the team who originally proposed, advocated, or led the change. This is not about rewarding failure, but rather about not punishing courage and innovation. Ideally, with the company culture behind you, a Noble Failure is a kind of neutral for your career: you don't advance, but you do survive professionally. It may even be a bit of a benefit, because you now have the experience of trying and failing and can apply that experience and the lessons learned to future projects. This concept is intended to encourage people to voice their opinions and ideas more freely because they know that even a failing effort will be tolerated, sometimes even celebrated, and never punished.

Early in my Schwab days we developed online trading software called the Equalizer (sadly, I am responsible for that corny name). No other discount trading firm had such a product and it garnered a small, very loyal following. It just wasn't user-friendly enough to attract a big and profitable client base. We learned from this experiment and years later replaced it with StreetSmart (better named by someone else), software that was based on an early version of Windows. This was much more successful, but it certainly wasn't a breakthrough. No one's career suffered for the lack of dramatic success with either of these software products. Instead, these efforts prepared us for the internet and we all learned what we needed to set ourselves up for online trading, which virtually reinvented Schwab. This was Noble Failure at its best.

~~~~~

Bringing initiatives to the real world is fraught with challenges. Even if you carefully and diligently follow and cycle back through the steps of the *Driving Disruption* process, negotiate terms, and consider the various issues and risks, you cannot guarantee success. Given the structure of organizations and the history of innovative change initiatives, the odds are almost always stacked against you. For the best possible chance of succeeding, you must combine a tested, thoughtful process and an experienced and skilled team of people with an extraordinary dose of authentic and inspiring leadership.

Scanning the Horizon for Innovation and Disruptive Change

INNOVATION IS BOTH INDISPENSABLE and inspiring. Initially, it often seems to come from a place beyond logic: a bright flash, an "aha! moment." By contrast, incremental changes are safe and generally straightforward; they bring steady improvement—to a point. They are not enough to reset the playing board, to rejigger where competitive advantage resides. Since truly transformative change needs innovation in the mix, how can we best find and nurture it?

The most valuable assets in our organizations are less about capital or existing products and more about the ability to be creative, to come up with innovative ideas, and to cultivate employee engagement and ownership of the future. For this, we need to enlist people's full engagement, their brains, and their passion. We need to encourage new ideas that help our organization succeed, to create the atmosphere in which new ideas can flourish, where managed risk is celebrated and where people can see their contributions to shared goals. The long-term strategic advantage is in having people at all levels believe that they can come up with new ideas to create new products and serve customers better—and that doing so can have long-reaching benefits.

How do we make the most of the combined intelligence of the people in our organizations? How do we keep the intelligence of the organization renewed and productive? What maintenance does the imagination require? In what atmosphere do innovation and employee engagement flourish? These are questions we must hold in mind as we build our culture, reinforce our purpose, and let our employees know how important they are to our future success. These are questions we must ask if we are to truly empower people to work together and bring their best ideas forward; for no one of us can be the source of all the new ideas and innovations we need, big and small.

Innovating by Meeting Unspoken and Undiscovered Needs

The best and most successful companies are adept at meeting needs that don't yet exist, or that exist at a low boil in the back of people's minds. If we are willing to declare a situation "good enough," we lose out on untold opportunities. Instead, innovation must be a constant. We must be willing to create a future out of nothing—and keep creating it. Successful innovators and those who strive to innovate are always looking for guidelines about where innovation comes from and how to mine those opportunities. Stay curious and you will find there are many paths.

Listen and Learn

Many of the best and most overlooked insights regarding innovation come from the people on the ground. There's simply no substitute for being out on the floor with employees and customers, talking face-to-face. Take the opportunities to listen, and you will learn where the problems are that could use your attention, for frontline employees and customers definitely know what works and what doesn't. Customers are very good at identifying their unmet needs and services or products they aren't getting from your business as it currently exists. Be sure that you and your organization's members are ready to listen to and act on what customers are telling you. In the best organizations, executives and marketing heads consistently interact directly with customers and discover innovative insights. When the executive team sets the benchmark by being present, this can ripple through the organization—and help ensure that innovation happens.

Similarly, companies benefit greatly when leaders seek out frontline employees and listen to their opinions and solutions. Sometimes what's needed are simply opportunities for customers and employees to speak with the organization's leaders. Be alert to those possibilities and create new ones when you can; actively engage and gather information all the time. You never know when your conversation or question might become the spark for an important innovation.

As an example, when I was at Schwab, I instituted regular monthly luncheons designed to gather and share information. We hosted 24 customers and 12 employees at each luncheon so that customers would receive individualized attention. The employees included a mix of very senior staff and those who led departments or units responsible for services, products, or policies. Customers who shared some important attribute would be invited to the same luncheon. One luncheon's attendees would be new customers from full-service firms with accounts above $250,000; another's would be customers with accounts above $250,000 who had just left us to go to full-service firms. Or it might be customers who had been with us for more than ten years or customers who traded more than 100 times a year. It was the passion behind the customers' words, the look in their eyes, the way they told their stories that gave us the information, perspective, and insight to take meaningful action. Customers were pleased to be heard and to see that we cared about their ideas and how we could improve our services; long-term, these interactions benefited everyone.

Ask Questions

Whether it's lunches, town hall meetings, or more informal interactions, shake people's hands and engage with them. Ask them critical questions: "What is not working for you right now? What are the pluses and the minuses of doing business with us? What are our competitors doing that we don't, and should?" Ask open-ended questions and high-gain questions, both of which provide information and keep the conversation flowing. Don't settle for yes or no answers; what you want are answers that provide new insights. And then follow up.

Simple as it sounds, asking questions is often one of the largest components of successful innovation. After you've laid some groundwork with customers, consider asking questions that might at first appear pie-in-the-sky, or even irrelevant: "What are your hopes and dreams right now? Absent any limits whatsoever, what would you want from our company?" Ask questions that help people look toward the future and think beyond the possible.

Be sure to ask similar questions of your team and your employees. And open yourself to possibility and innovation by asking yourself, "If there were no limits, what would I like our business to do?" Challenge yourself, and others, with bold questions. Bold questions—and bold answers—bring dramatic results.

Jim Collins, author of multiple best-selling business books, has an excellent concept that gets to the foundation of answering big, bold questions: Always look for the "and" answer, not the "or" answer. Too often, leaders will say things like, "We must choose between great customer service or low prices." Instead, why not figure out a way to offer both? That kind of open-ended thinking can keep you from being hamstrung by the accepted wisdom about what is and what is not possible and can open up entirely new avenues. It's a concept that is now so well understood that car advertisements build on it, promoting the idea that buyers no longer have to choose between great gas mileage or a fun car, but can have both—in one vehicle.

If you want to innovate, don't fall into the trap of thinking that the status quo is good enough. It can be changed—and that's an opportunity.

Tying Innovations to Values

Leaders understand that success can breed complacency, and that's especially true when it comes to innovation. When you have been successful for a long time, it's hard to resist the temptation to play it safe and focus on incremental improvements. You have an existing technology, distribution system, sales structure, or product line. Why bother operating outside of that framework or reinventing what's working? Undertaking something new is difficult, particularly when the benefits of implementing it are unclear or unproven; even more so when the drawbacks and barriers are obvious.

A new product line may well erode the sales of your existing products. Before you decide whether you are willing to take that kind of risk, recognize that it's a risk either way, since companies that resist adding products that might eat into their existing sales often wind up leaving a gap in the market that a competitor soon exploits. What then is the better choice?

It's always tough to leave a comfortable present for an uncertain future, and it's not just tough on leadership. You can make this process easier by grounding the innovation within your culture. When you talk about what is changing, be sure to remind everyone what is *not* changing as well.

Process, procedure, and product are the elements of a business that most commonly undergo regular changes. In many cases, these are constantly changing in incremental or in bold ways. By contrast, a company's big-picture strategy might change only once every five to ten years; and the company's core mission, purpose, and even its overarching strategies generally remain stable over time. There are good reasons for this: core beliefs ground people and let new and long-term employees know what the company is all about.

In describing a new process, procedure, or product, contextualize it alongside the company's core values. Yes, you might say, this new product could chip away at sales for some of our other products, but it is wonderfully consistent with who we are as a company. We should all be comfortable with the idea of this product as an important part of our client proposition. Connecting the new change with the old values makes the change less daunting for everyone (except perhaps the team assigned to drive the sales of the older product, but this is manageable and reasonable to expect).

Further, if your organization embraces the concept of Noble Failure (discussed in Step Eight), the fear surrounding innovation is defused and innovations flow more freely. And in today's hypercompetitive world, nothing less than courageous leadership and innovative, disruptive changes will do.

Breakthroughs Ahead

Sometimes the situation you are confronted with calls for a leap of faith. What if no matter how carefully or creatively you crunch the numbers, there is little evidence to prove that your approach will provide the outcome you want with a degree of certainty that would make your CFO smile? What if you see opportunities that others can't yet imagine? These can be the scariest innovations of all—and may also have the most potential.

Then there are the leaps of faith you must take in your business in responding to threats that you can see but that have barely begun to register in the metrics or in your organization's awareness. No one can predict the future with any certainty, but what is certain is that it will bring new challenges and demands. So, you carefully evaluate the path you are on. You know that the current path won't lead to the success you need, but those around you are telling you to play it safe, to wait and see if things really do get worse. But you see what your competitors are doing, and your gut, fueled by the knowledge and experience you've acquired over time, is telling you that if you don't innovate, your competitors' positions will—over time, and maybe not much time—erode your own. If you find that you have to do something bold, then you will. By using the steps in *Driving Disruption,* you can prepare yourself and your team as you move forward into that bold, innovative change.

Not a single one of the steps is easy. Recognizing a need to change is hard, assembling a team is hard, piloting is hard. What is easy is getting discouraged, getting disillusioned. It's very easy to think the difficulties you encounter must be your fault, that you must have screwed something up because nothing should be this hard. But disruptive change *is* that hard—as it should be. It's actually good for the process to be difficult. This is the crucible where substantial competitive advantage and economic value are created. Do not be discouraged by the difficulties ahead. These are opportunities to challenge yourself and the rewards will be greater for the effort. You're not alone: even the most successful change leaders struggle and even their most successful initiatives demanded extraordinary effort.

In the right hands, and with the right mind-set, the steps can help you create a more productive and readily navigated path through disruptive change. The process itself is less about *what* to think than *how* to think. It's about learning to anticipate and to analyze logically and carefully; thinking creatively and embracing possibilities; learning what to prioritize, where to concentrate energy, and how to move forward while bringing others along with you.

And there's the key: Leaders bring people along. When a clear process is in place, people get energized; they know where they're going and what to do. But the process alone won't meet with success. Instead, it's the combination of ongoing inspiration—the mark of true leadership—with the structure and discipline of the steps and the assembly of a talented team that creates enormous advantages for a change effort. It is my deepest hope that the material and suggestions provided in this workbook will encourage you and help you succeed as you take on disruptive, innovative changes and the vast possibilities of the future.

ACKNOWLEDGMENTS

THANKS TO THE STUDENTS in the Wharton Executive MBA program who have embraced my teachings with enthusiasm and made clear to me the need for this book. Steeped as these emerging leaders are in the pace of change, they want a short, practical guide to help them move quickly into driving disruptive change. Rather than just suggest and move on, many of them also offered detailed recommendations and reviewed drafts along the way. These students and the corporate leaders with whom I consult throughout the year constantly inspire me to keep learning and growing. Thank you all.

As my teaching assistant for the past several years, Mike Gipe has been invaluable to me and to the success of the class. Teaching without his help and support is not something I want to imagine. Nate Jewell, a former student and now a good friend, has actively contributed from the very beginning. My heartfelt thanks to you both.

Acknowledging the entire team that put together *Driving Disruption* requires deep bows in many directions. There are, of course, all the accomplished leaders I initially interviewed for my previous book, *Stacking the Deck*. These leaders, none of whom have empty blocks on their calendars, generously shared their experiences, knowledge, and insights with me and helped me expand my thoughts. In addition, I've been lucky enough to tap a wide range of leaders as guest presenters in the classes I teach for the Wharton Executive MBA program. To date, nearly 20 leaders have shared their experiences there. You know who you are. What you may not know is how deeply I value your involvement and the degree to which the class—as individuals and as a group—is inspired by your presence and perspectives.

As is made clear in this book's opening chapters, my debt to Terry Pearce cannot be measured in bows or words. Long since named the "éminence grise" of executive coaches, Terry embodies authenticity—in leadership communication and in life. I count myself lucky to be one of his pupils.

The luck continues. Terry introduced me to Jan Hunter, who has been my developmental editor on each of my books. As always, I'm grateful for her clarity, knowledge, and general counsel. Her contributions continue to exceed my expectations of what an editor delivers to the process, product, and team.

Creating a workbook led me to a new adventure in publishing, with yet another team. Book designer and all-around publishing expert Dick Margulis carried this book from its final draft to the practical workbook you have in your hands. His expertise and calm direction deserve more praise than we have room for here. Thanks, too, to Katharine Wiencke and Marilyn Augst, the skilled proofreader and indexer Dick brought in to complete the job.

Alexandra Kealy deserves boundless credit for keeping me on track, pointed in the right direction, and productive as I attempt to juggle the demands of boards, businesses, and life.

Back in 1990, I was incredibly fortunate to cross paths with Colleen Bagan, who helped me absorb and complete the myriad demands of my positions at Schwab. My good fortune has lasted through the decades, as she continues to make me look good, professionally and personally, in all spheres of my life. I know it isn't easy, and yet she makes it seem so. I'm delighted to acknowledge my eternal thanks and gratitude for her presence in my life.

DAVID S. POTTRUCK is the former CEO of Charles Schwab. Dave joined the Charles Schwab Corporation in 1984 as Executive Vice President of Marketing and led its innovative direct response advertising campaigns. Under his marketing leadership from 1984 to 1987, when the company went public, Schwab's revenues tripled in size. He became Schwab's President and COO in 1992, co-CEO with Chuck Schwab in 1998, and CEO in 2002. Over Dave's 20-year tenure at Schwab, the company's assets in custody grew from $5 billion to over $1 trillion and the equity value of Schwab grew from roughly $50 million to approximately $16 billion.

During Dave's leadership, Schwab refocused its business model entirely on the internet, a radically transformative move that drove the company's explosive growth. Schwab also led a reinvention of the no-load mutual fund industry with the introduction of the no-fee "mutual fund supermarket" concept and introduced the RIA servicing business; both innovations are now cornerstones of the discount brokerage industry.

This RIA experience was invaluable when Dave became a founding investor in HighTower Advisors, helping it grow from an idea to a thriving business with over $50 billion in assets, nearly 100 locations, and over 500 employees. He served on HighTower's board and as the chair for close to a decade, stepping down as it was sold in 2018.

Dave served on the Board of Directors of Intel Corporation from 1998 to 2018, and was a member of the Executive Committee, Chairman of the Compensation Committee, and Chairman of the Retirement Plan Investment Committee. He is on the Board of Directors of GSV Capital, a publicly traded investment fund that gives growth equity investors access to private companies with huge potential. He also advises the CEOs of several early-stage companies. Dave was formerly a Trustee of the University of Pennsylvania and Chair of the San Francisco Committee on Jobs.

Dave is the coauthor with Terry Pearce of *Clicks and Mortar: Passion-Driven Growth in an Internet-Driven World*. A top-ten best seller in *BusinessWeek* and on Amazon, *Clicks and Mortar* has been translated into six languages. In Dave's second book, *Stacking the Deck: How to Lead Breakthrough Change Against Any Odds*, a New York Times best seller, Dave synthesized his and other leaders' experiences to help executives increase the likelihood of success.

He is a Senior Fellow and adjunct faculty member at the Wharton School's Center for Leadership and Change Management. In 2010 and again in 2012, he received Wharton San Francisco's Outstanding Teaching Award. Dave has delivered keynote speeches and taught change leadership to hundreds of executives from around the world.

Dave has received accolades and recognition from numerous organizations and publications. He has been named one of the "Top 15 CEOs" by *Worth*; "CEO of the Year" by *InformationWeek*; "Executive of the Year" by the *San Francisco Business Times*; and "CEO of the Year" by Morningstar. He was named by *SmartMoney* as one of the three most influential executives in the world of investing and by *Institutional Investor* as the number one most influential executive in the world of online finance.

In 1999 he was appointed by Congress and then-President Clinton to serve as one of 19 Commissioners on the Advisory Commission on Electronic Commerce, which was tasked with producing recommendations on electronic commerce and tax policy, arguably one of the most important policy initiatives of the Information Age.

Dave graduated with a BA from the University of Pennsylvania and earned his MBA with honors from Wharton.

INDEX

WHAT'S NEXT, NOW THAT you've read the manual? You'll need time for reflection and the inner work required to become an effective and authentic leader. And you'll need unending passion, commitment, and inspiration to see your change through.

If you've accessed the links at the end of the steps, you know there's more information than just the action items available on the book's website.

www.DrivingDisruption.com

Our goal for *Driving Disruption* was a portable, easily used guide to planning and executing disruptive change. Short and succinct were the watchwords. For that, we had to leave a wealth of stories and details on the cutting room floor. Many of those stories will appear on the website. Browse through and see; come back periodically and see what's new.

The website includes brief summaries of the chapters of part one, links to relevant articles, a list of the leaders interviewed, and recommended readings. It also provides a forum for input and questions. So, if you want more on a particular topic or step; if you have any questions, comments, or stories to offer, just use the Contact Us link to send a note.

You can also conveniently download a copy of the E-book via the site.

Here's to your future successes!